RISK TO WIN

Also by Jeannette R. Scollard

The Self-Employed Woman:
How to Start Your Own Business and
Gain Control of Your Life

No-Nonsense Management Tips for
Women

RISK TO WIN

A Woman's Guide to Success

JEANNETTE R. SCOLLARD

Macmillan Publishing Company
New York

Collier Macmillan Publishers
London

Macmillan Publishing Company
866 Third Avenue, New York, NY 10022
Collier Macmillan Canada, Inc.

Library of Congress Cataloging-in-Publication Data
Scollard, Jeannette Reddish.
   Risk to win: a woman's guide to success/Jeannette R. Scollard.
      p. cm.
   Includes index.
   ISBN 0-02-608551-8
      1. Women—Psychology.   2. Risk-taking (Psychology)   3. Success.
I. Title.
HQ1206.S445   1989   89-2741   CIP
158'.1—dc19

Macmillan books are available at special discounts for bulk purchases for sales promotions, premiums, fund-raising, or educational use. For details, contact:

Special Sales Director
Macmillan Publishing Company
866 Third Avenue
New York, NY 10022

10 9 8 7 6 5 4 3 2

Designed by Jack Meserole

PRINTED IN THE UNITED STATES OF AMERICA

To my father, who reminds me
that everything is possible.

Contents

Contents

Foreword

YOU HAVE to take risks to succeed. Risks are part of any changes you initiate in your business or personal life. You risk when you adapt, modify, improve, or innovate. You risk whether you like it or not. There is no way to avoid risk taking. Indeed, to choose not to take a risk is often the greatest risk.

A risk is what you experience any time you move forward or take an action where you cannot guarantee its ramifications and outcome. There is risk entailed in every action you take. Risk taking is an essential part of being alive.

But you can manage your risks. You can learn how to pick your risks. You can learn how to take bigger risks. You can learn how to take risks better. How to take the right risk at the right time and achieve your objective. Risk taking does not have to be foolhardy. The degree of exposure to injury or loss is up to you. If you train all your life to be a trapeze artist, your chances of falling are far less than the chances of someone who has never prepared and does it on a dare.

You can choose your risks. You can time them. You can measure them. You can research them.

There are foolish risks and there are intelligent ones. It is up to you to do your homework and decide which you are facing. Research your odds for success, talk to people and evaluate the up side and the down side. Then listen to your gut and proceed. It's up to you.

This book will show you how.

Acknowledgments

THIS BOOK is possible because of the encouragement and support I received from a host of people. At the top of the list is Terry Lust, my capable assistant, who toiled long and hard to help me complete it. Her loyalty and grace inspire us all. I also want to acknowledge the resourcefulness of Donna Barnett, who helped me research *Risk to Win*. It also wouldn't have been possible without the generous moral support lent by the always generous Bridget McGonigle. I also want to thank Judith Moncrieff for her belief in me, Merry Clark for her encouragement, and John Mabry for cheering me on. And special thanks to Alicia Fox, Nikki Frost, Judith Jones, Roxandra Antoniadis, Gloria Wise, and Marietta Paladin.

I particularly want to thank Lenny Thompson for his kindness and assistance to me throughout this project. His help was invaluable.

RISK TO WIN

1

Men and Women
Are Different

THE WORD *risk* conjures up a variety of responses. Generally women find the word menacing. And men find it appealing and sexy. What's the difference?

A lot of it is the word. It's a very male word. And men have long been touted as the risk takers of our culture. The genderization begins early on. For instance, little girls who climb trees are called tomboys because it's considered risky to climb trees and little girls don't take those risks.

In my lectures I sometimes throw the word *risk* out and ask my audience what the word means to them. Men usually answer, "Opportunity" or "Success." Women, on the other hand, frequently respond, "Fear" or "Failure."

Whether the reasons that men and women perceive risks differently are cultural or biological is not something that *Risk to Win* will attempt to explore. We will deal with the facts as they are: Risk taking is viewed differently by men and women.

MEN AND RISK TAKING

"There is more foolhardiness in men," observes Ralph Hirschowitz, a Boston psychiatrist and Harvard professor. Hirschowitz feels that our "frontier heritage" has been a factor in the attitude men have toward risk taking. Consider the elements of a typical

John Wayne movie. Wayne is the powerful macho risk taker. He stands up and shoots a gun, taking the ultimate risk—his life. The women in his movie are usually victims, pawns of circumstance, certainly incapable of standing up and shooting it out with the villain. They are decent, resourceful women, but in dreadful need of a protector to go out and take the risks for them so that they can continue to tend to home and hearth. The biggest risk the women in these movies usually take is in falling in love with the hero.

His macho risk taking makes the hero sexier than he would otherwise be. The woman wants the security of having him around the homestead to continue taking risks. She will risk marrying him, bearing his children—major personal risks. But the business risks—the business of gunslinging—she leaves up to him.

Often things haven't changed very much. Part of the macho culture is still physical risk taking—settling an argument with their fists, for instance.

And the macho language of sports risk taking has been brought in by men to dramatize the risks they take in business. The language adds a physicality to the risk taking. Moreover, the language of war has been brought into the boardroom to add the drama of combat to the risk taking.

War and sports are male domains. So is the business world—to a great extent. By bringing their vocabulary to risk taking, men have brought some of the excitement of the battlefield and sports arena to glorify the risks of business. And incidentally, that vocabulary makes business risk taking even more intimidating to women.

Can you imagine if the tables were turned and we women brought some of the language of our traditional arena—home and hearth—to the business world? How much less intimidating the risks would be if we had phrases such as:

Chopped, minced, and diced the competition
Threw them in the food processor
Start off with a clean diaper

It's hard to imagine. There are very few phrases that have made it from the household into business risk taking. One such is "throw out the baby with the bathwater." But, by and large, the vocabulary bears a heavy macho orientation. Even "a clean sweep" and "mop up" came from the male culture—from men taking care of ships and the bunkhouse.

RISK–TAKING LANGUAGE: Sitting Tall in the Saddle in the Boardroom

---

Throw a fastball	Win the battle, lose the war
Up at bat	Captain
Designated hitter	Team
Up at bat with the bases loaded	Major assault
Full-court press	Call in the second team
Go into a huddle	Team player
Run with the ball	Foul ball
Score a touchdown	Direct hit
Score	Knock-down drag-out fight
Double team	Referee
Out of bounds	Chief
First down	Launch a major offensive
Warroom	Minefields
Ammunition	Down in the trenches
Armed to the teeth	Under heavy fire
Patrol	Rank-and-file
Catching flak	Fight a good battle
Full artillery	War zone
Mexican standoff	A clean sweep
Rally the troops	A mop-up operation

The physical orientation of the language of risk taking reflects an essential male preoccupation with brute strength. There is a warrior mentality. "Men are brave. Women don't want to be brave," posits the male editor of a New York City–based newspaper. "Women don't appreciate bravery. But you must be brave to be a risk taker. Women don't comprehend bravery. They think it's foolishness," he adds.

The warrior mentality is connected to physical strength. "I don't know how women would get it. When you're 115 pounds you can't handle 200," says a former football player who feels bravery stems from confidence. "When I played football I never worried about being hurt. The athlete who thinks like this never gets hurt," maintains the jock who also believes that knowing you are tough and fit physically affects your ability to take risks. "Men lead physically as much as mentally," he notes. "I don't know if women can do that."

Men typically consider only themselves to be the risk takers in our culture. Sam Metters, who heads up his own systems research and development firm, says women are "afraid" to take risks. "The forum in which you're forced to try to succeed is not conducive to success. This is a man's world. And regardless if people try to change that, it's not going to happen. Moreover, it cannot happen because we need to maintain the status quo." He continues, "Women are more adaptive within their domain. Men are more innovative. They break through their domain. They then come back to reality by the woman drawing them back. The woman is the regulator—the maintainer of the status quo."

Metters is typical in his assessment of the risk-taking ability of women. When you talk to many men, they are proud of their own ability to take risks. For instance, producer Michael Linder says that he likes the television business because of its instability. "Everything is a short-term phenomenon, where there are no long-term positions. A show may come and go and last a year or two. This suits me just fine, because the last thing I want to do is be someone crystallized in any one job, one role or one circumstance." The challenge of it inspires him. "Every job I've ever had was to kick off something new and innovative from scratch," Linder continues. His risk taking is a life-style. "I do take risks in my personal life. I love sports. I ride motorcycles all over the continent, and this week I'm going out with some vice cops in D.C. to go on some busts. They're taking me along as one of them, and I crave that excitement and danger."

So, you see that men do not expect women to be risk takers. Indeed, many of them think we are incapable of taking risks. And you see that underlying men's attitudes about risk taking there is a machismo, a sexual bias. It is as though you have to be a rugged six-footer with bulging muscles to have the ability to take risks. It is as though you have to be able to "get it up" to qualify for risk taking.

Men see themselves as the warriors and see us as the docile keepers of the house and hearth. They innovate, and we adapt. They create, and we sustain.

We are constantly being bombarded with this attitude. No wonder that women are put off even by the word *risk*. We're still being told, on the threshold of the twenty-first century, that we simply don't have what it takes to be risk takers.

SCOLLARD'S LAW   The warrior mentality is in no way an essential characteristic of a successful risk taker.

WOMEN AND RISK TAKING

It's clear that women are not expected by our male counterparts to take risks. The prevalent attitudes about our limitations have affected the way we view ourselves and our abilities. We're being told that we can't be brave, that we are a separate species.

In fact, we take risks all the time, but we do not view them in those terms. Getting married and having children are two of the biggest risks you could possibly take. Yet we women blithely do these things. We just don't view them as risks. We have been successfully brainwashed. We do in fact view risk taking as something that is dangerous, something to avoid.

Obviously women are capable of taking business risks, although since men expect them not to, it may be more difficult for us to break through the cultural conditioning. Four million women have their own businesses, and entrepreneurship is the essence of risk taking. Millions of women are working in corporate America, changing jobs, and jockeying for promotions—more risk taking.

What we need to do is to deliberately develop our risk-taking skills. We also need to overcome the prejudice against us. If men do not believe women are capable of risk taking, we are put in the situation of having to prove ourselves. Men, on the other hand, have the old-boy network and popular opinion reinforcing them as they forge ahead.

We're still our own worst enemies, asking permission from the men around us. So, we have to start at home, educating our fathers and our husbands about our risk-taking abilities. Observes Mobil executive Judith Moncrieff, "Women are more other-oriented. They worry about how it's going to affect Mom, the kids. Women take too much responsibility for everything around them. They need to focus on becoming self-confident, focus on their self-confidence muscles much as a runner trains for a marathon."

And the world is slowly changing. The warrior mentality is being challenged by women who are taking risks in the same arena as men. Women like Asa Miller are discovering they can take risks and succeed. Miller says she started her advertising and marketing business with "nothing in place. I didn't have confidence." She started the business with her husband, who unfortunately became ill, forcing her to run everything on her own until he recovered.

DISCRIMINATION

The barriers women face in the marketplace are real. One is discrimination. The assumption is made that we *choose* to work whereas men *have* to work. "This assumption is not borne out in reality," says Jacqueline D. Goodchilds, an associate profes-sor in the psychology department at UCLA. Most women work because they need the money and because they find it fulfilling—the same reasons that men work. People still assume that women have a choice about whether they marry and stay home or they work. "This is not a real choice for people," says Goodchilds.

Discrimination against women is dying a slow death. It just doesn't go away. To succeed in corporate America, you have to be better than most of your male counterparts. This is because the incompetent male managers are frequently protected by their peers in the old-boy network. Women have no such network. We are typically excluded completely from the old-boy network. We don't socialize with them. We don't go out to dinner with them. We don't play tennis or golf with them. So there is no one to protect a woman who is mediocre. One woman tells of a male colleague she worked with who had a drug problem, a drinking problem, a temper problem, and who was discovered in an act of sexual intercourse with a female intern on a desktop after office hours. "This man was promoted," observes the woman executive. "If a woman ever did half of what he did, she'd be out on her ass. And he gets promoted!"

Notes Hearst Corporation executive Merry Clark, "It's ex-tremely difficult when women are in management. Men are afraid women will take over the turf. Men are very territorial. Women don't get a chance to show what they can do."

If you're in a situation where you feel discrimination, there are things you can do. Change jobs. Not all companies have the same level of discrimination. Maybe you should take a bigger risk and change industries. Fashion, advertising, and consumer products have far more opportunities for women than other in-dustries do.

Discrimination is a way of life. There's little we can do to combat it except to be excellent at what we do and win respect. Study the career strategies discussed in chapter 6 and risk changing jobs to further your career around the obstacles in your path.

SCOLLARD'S LAW Corporate America was designed by men for men. Women were executive wives relegated to bedrooms and kitchens. It will take generations before women are accepted in the boardroom.

SELF–IMPOSED LIMITATIONS

There is not much we can do about discrimination, but our self-imposed limitations are another matter. We *can* do something about them. We *can* learn to take more risks. And this book can show you how.

We are often too tentative, too cautious. One male executive confided to me that the three women who report to him are far less adventurous and innovative than the men who work for him. "A woman is always asking permission," he observed. "They always want to know exactly what their boundaries are, exactly what is expected of them. The men don't ask those kinds of questions. They explore their boundaries on their own. For that reason they are often more effective in uncharted development."

But we do have one great advantage over men. We have our intuition, but often we're afraid to use it. Don't be. Take it to work with you and rely on it. A woman's highly trained sensibilities can be a tremendous asset in corporate politics and game playing.

We women have trouble with our self-esteem, too. Women's magazines pander to our weaknesses. They have articles that make us uncomfortable with where we are at the time. Is it time to have children? Are you neglecting your children? Are your hips too big? Is your husband having an affair? Are you seductive enough? Should you restyle your hair? We read these magazines and doubt ourselves. Men don't read these things. They don't worry about their hips and their hairstyle on a daily basis. Men read *Forbes*. They read *Fortune*. They don't spend their time second-guessing themselves. They read things that apply to their business. They don't worry about the same things we do.

Perhaps we should take a lesson from men and stop worrying about these things, too. We should consciously work on raising our self-esteem. "The only woman's magazine I read is *House and Garden*," says one successful woman. "Everything else I read has to do with current affairs or business. I'm certainly not interested in reading about my sexual quotient. I can figure that out myself."

Women are also tempted to make decisions based on what people will think rather than relying on themselves. "I find that many women suffer from the wanting-to-please syndrome," says a California executive. "They say, 'What would people think if I took this risk?' Men tend to be more certain of their own judgment." Again we should learn from men. Pam Fletcher-Hafemann, a successful entrepreneur in Oceanside, California, says, "Men project confidence. Women don't. They vacillate more. They think, 'Well, maybe . . .'"

Take the risk. Make the decision based on your own common sense. The worst thing that can happen is that you will be wrong.

Also, we are not aggressive enough about asking. We don't ask for the raise or the opportunity to get the tough project that will lead to a promotion. A lot of women expect raises and promotions to be handed to them. That isn't the way the system works. You have to go after it.

Here we have to be careful. There is a fine line in men's perceptions between being a go-getter and being a pushy broad. Use your intuition to assess how you are being perceived. It's a fine line to walk. And sometimes you can't win, because any assertiveness will be interpreted negatively. In that case, get another job where you will be able to forge ahead.

Finally, because we have to work harder to be successful, we become less capable than men of accepting success. They take raises and bonuses as expected and just rewards. We women tend to be less comfortable with success. We feel grateful. We repay with too much loyalty.

DIFFERENCES BETWEEN
MEN AND WOMEN

1. When something goes wrong at the office, HE looks for whom to blame; SHE wonders, "What did I do wrong?"
2. The boss goes on a rampage. HE thinks, "I'll bet the old man completely forgets about this tomorrow." SHE thinks, "I hope I don't get fired."
3. They get raises. HE thinks, "It should be more. Maybe I can swing the bonus." SHE thinks, "I'm lucky my boss went to bat for me."
4. When HE can't find his pants in the morning, he asks HER. She finds them for him. SHE can't find her belt, but HE doesn't hear her when she mentions the fact.
5. When there is a problem at school involving their child, the teacher automatically calls HER.
6. SHE picks out the linens for the table.
7. HER raise is less than his.
8. HE runs into the president on the golf course on Saturday. They discuss a deal under consideration briefly.
9. At a restaurant the waiter takes the check automatically to her male client—even though the reservation was in HER name.
10. HE uses the executive john, where he runs into the CEO. SHE uses the one used by the secretaries and the switchboard operator.
11. SHE doesn't dare drink more than two cocktails. HE goes out and ties one on with the boys.
12. When HE gets married, it is viewed as a sign of maturity and commitment. When SHE gets married, everyone starts watching her waistline.
13. When they have children, HE is viewed as showing responsibility and maturity; SHE is watched for signs of losing her competitive edge.
14. When SHE has children, her commitment is for eighteen

years. When HE has children, his commitment is until the divorce.

15. SHE has a perfect résumé. The only problem is that her name is a woman's.

16. When HE's grouchy, his employees assume he's overworked. When SHE's grouchy, they assume it's her period.

2

Are You a Natural

Risk Taker?

IT IS QUESTIONABLE whether anyone is born a risk taker. It is likely that you become one through the experiences of your life, through trial and error. Some people learn to take risks at a younger age, because their home environment encourages—or forces—them to. But anyone can train himself or herself to become a member of that separate breed. A very special breed. Not necessarily any better than the rest of human kind. But decidedly different.

The difference is not visible to the eye at first glance. The difference is not necessarily external—although when you see someone in astonishing clothes and purple hair, you might well assume that you're looking at a risk taker. On the other hand, some of the most daring and courageous risk takers I've met didn't look any different from the most timid, conventional, and unambitious person I might encounter.

They don't *look* different. But you may well sense something different about the way they act. The risk taker will very likely project self-confidence and enthusiasm for her work. She will have a different attitude—very likely more positive than many people you meet.

This attitude is a result of having faced life head on—and won. Maybe those challenges were met with fear and misgivings, but more importantly, they were met with resolve and determination.

When we consider becoming risk takers ourselves, we need first to analyze what characteristics most successful risk takers embody. You can break them down into four categories: Passion, Honor, Creativity, and Charm. Not all risk takers have all of these. But all successful risk takers have some of them.

You should study these categories and see how you measure up. If you find yourself coming up short in some areas, don't be discouraged: Risk takers are usually not born that way. They become that way. They develop over time.

You can become a risk taker, too. You can change yourself. You can develop your strengths and overcome your shortcomings over a period of time. I, for instance, am on a continuing campaign to improve my own risk-taking quotient. Each year I tackle a few different characteristics I want to develop or eliminate. It is an endless battle.

SCOLLARD'S LAW   The successful risk taker is always looking for her next challenge. That's how she gets her kicks.

PASSION

The one attribute characteristic of all successful risk takers is passion. This is a completely positive passion, a compelling desire to succeed accompanied by an emotional intensity. It is a passion that is focused so positively that it excludes negative passions, such as rage and revenge. Instead you find in risk takers a passionate commitment to their goals and a harnessed excitement about their efforts. Says Lynn Loring, executive vice president of MGM/UA Television Productions, "At the heart of everything is an enormous passion for what I do."

This passion manifests itself in a wide variety of traits common to many of the most successful risk takers. It is this passion that fuels their progress and propels them toward the realization of their goals.

TEST YOUR PASSION

	YES	NO
1. I worry that the national economy is in a steep decline.	___	___
2. I worry that the area of business I am interested in is in an economic downturn.	___	___
3. Changes in my life should be made slowly.	___	___
4. I need a great deal of emotional support.	___	___
5. To accomplish a great deal, I rely on my friends to inspire me.	___	___
6. I can do things without any help from anyone.	___	___
7. I do the best I can. If it isn't perfect, I can live with it.	___	___
8. It's okay to procrastinate doing some things. Some tasks go away if you put them off long enough.	___	___
9. My husband has to push me out of bed in the morning. I hate to get up.	___	___
10. My goal is to be able to delegate everything and live a life of ease.	___	___
11. Money is a primary motivation. I can learn to love any business that pays enough.	___	___
12. I recognize my limitations. If I'm not good at something, I give it up and try something else.	___	___
13. I have a fitness program I adhere to regularly.	___	___
14. If my husband/boyfriend doesn't call me, it ruins my day.	___	___
15. I could never let my friends see how eccentric I really am.	___	___
16. I want to be the very best. This is far more important than making money.	___	___

YES   NO

17. Making money is not enough. I want to be respected. ____ ____

18. How my family regards my business influences how I conduct it. ____ ____

19. When I accomplish a certain level of success, I plan to retire and become a full-time housewife. ____ ____

20. If my husband/boyfriend and I disagree about my risk taking, I reconsider my original decision. ____ ____

21. Without the support of my family I could not be who I am. ____ ____

22. The harder the task, the more I like it. ____ ____

23. I think I can do the impossible. ____ ____

24. I have worked twelve-hour days that felt as though they were only an hour long. ____ ____

25. If I work, I like to work hard. ____ ____

26. I am unhappy with my life, but my friends say I am crazy to think of changing it. They may be right. ____ ____

27. I don't need to set an alarm to awaken at six to prepare for an important meeting. ____ ____

28. I am by nature a happy person. ____ ____

29. Work agrees with me. ____ ____

30. Hard work agrees with me even more. ____ ____

31. I feel I should conform to what my friends and colleagues expect of me. ____ ____

32. I don't rock the boat if it isn't necessary. ____ ____

33. Emotional turmoil devastates my work performance. ____ ____

34. I've never been shy about asking men to dance. ____ ____

35. There isn't anything I can't do if I set my mind to it. ____ ____

SCORES:

Perfect score: 35. Score one point for each correct answer.

Answer yes to   3, 6, 13, 16, 17, 22, 23, 24, 25, 27, 28, 29, 30, 34, 35.

Answer no to all others.

30–35   You have great passion and are a natural risk taker.

22–29   You can easily develop your risk-taking inclinations.

15–21   You will need to study this chapter carefully and train yourself to become a risk taker.

15 and below   You lack self-confidence and independence and should begin a campaign to strengthen your resolve and trust yourself more.

Optimism. A positive, can-do attitude is essential to successful risk taking. It is as though you could *will* the desired outcome to occur. You must believe that you can achieve what you aspire to. The glass is always half full and never half empty to the successful risk taker. You see the best possible outcome of taking a risk. You understand the down side and the possibility of failure. But what you focus on is the opportunity for success.

This optimism is pervasive. It has to do not only with personal success but with an attitude toward life in general. A successful risk taker finds plenty of blessings to count and counts them unabashedly. Patricia Harrison, a single mother of three who started her own business, is typical when she says "This is the best of all possible times. Because this is the time. We're not at war with anybody. We don't have to worry about that. The economy is good." Harrison continues. "I don't mean to sound like a Pollyanna, because I'm a realist. But I'm grateful every single day that I wasn't born in Afghanistan and sweeping the street—anything is up from that point. I hope my kids feel the same way. I think they do." She adds, "Enough already with the whining and the crying. I think sometimes we don't focus on what we have."

The risk-taker mentality naturally views risks positively. Sally Marshall, a television producer, comments, "Risk taking means respecting fear but not being afraid to jump into it. There isn't anything you can't do, and nothing is ever lost." A successful entrepreneur agrees, "Risk taking means taking a calculated risk to get something that can be many times greater than not taking that move." Adds Rebecca Tilton, "I enjoy going against everyone saying, 'You're not going to make it. The economy is bad.' I'm a very optimistic person."

When risk takers talk, almost always it's the up side they emphasize. The down side is not their favorite topic of conversation. Successful risk takers are not easily discouraged or deterred. They make things happen. They *will* things to happen. They thrive on adversity and raise their adrenaline by taking on challenges. And after they've met one challenge, they typically seek out the next hurdle. They frequently succeed in circumstances in which the sages and pundits are solemnly prophesying doom. This country was built by people who paid no attention while their detractors predicted, "It won't work. It's a crazy idea."

SCOLLARD'S LAW The difficult takes a day to accomplish. The impossible takes a little bit longer—but not a lot.

Determination. Successful risk takers are not easily discouraged. They seize the opportunity and single-mindedly go for it.

"I don't give up," says realtor Nancy Helmer. "I'm persistent." She is typical of the tenacity risk takers often exhibit. With dogged persistence they make things happen. Accomplishing the difficult is commonplace. The "impossible" is quite doable. "I didn't let anyone stand in my way. I went for it," relates the 1988 Miss America. "I knew where I wanted to go and I worked hard enough, and it came true."

Many people are content to give a project their best effort and then philosophically accept defeat if their efforts are in vain. Not risk takers. They stick with a project until their expectations are met. The attitude is that almost anything is possible if you really want to do it. Says Lynn Loring, "I've always believed that if I want something badly enough, I can have it. So the question is, 'How badly do I want it?'"

Successful risk takers turn a deaf ear to people who discourage them, who continually warn them of the difficulties and obstacles in their path. They are unwilling to expend the energy to explain themselves to those who do not share their vision. Instead they seek out positive people who cheer them on. Or they fight their battle for success all alone.

SCOLLARD'S LAW   Trying to talk a risk taker out of pursuing her own vision of success is harder than persuading a hungry bulldog to let go of its favorite bone.

Impatience. Risk takers don't wait for the world to come to them. They mount a campaign to take it. On their own terms. In their own time frame. A risk taker will demonstrate the patience of Job when it comes to executing her strategy, but it was impatience that activated her strategy in the first place. Comments one executive who is now actively considering the possibility of leaving corporate America and starting her own business, "Impatience to get ahead is a motivating factor."

SCOLLARD'S LAW   A risk taker is an impatient gardener. She is anxious to rush the season and plant the seed, but must accept that once it takes root it has its own innate schedule.

SCOLLARD'S LAW   If you turn a hair dryer on a rosebud, you can force it to open before its time.

Self-motivation. The risk taker is aware that the chances of a guardian angel intervening and putting her life on track are nil. She aggressively takes charge of her future well-being. She accepts responsibility for her life and her destiny—*con gusto.* "I do have tremendous drive," observes Carol Highsmith, who chucked an eighteen-year career in broadcasting and decided to become a photographer. "It's like I was sucked into a moment of history."

Once the decision to take a certain course has been made, the successful risk taker knows the responsibility is hers to execute the plan of action successfully. "I think to start a business like I did, you have to be a self-starter," notes a Northeast attorney, who with a partner founded a law firm. "You can't just wait for someone to come to you. You have to reach out and makes things happen, and I was able to do those things."

To be successful, you have to drive yourself. The burden is yours. No one else will care about your success as much as you. Typically you will be so excited about important meetings that you will awaken in the morning without needing an alarm clock.

SCOLLARD'S LAW You can increase your motivation by watching the success others are achieving. If they can do it, can't you do it better?

Independence. For the typical business person there is a tremendous sense of pressure to conform to the status quo, to remain in the docile mainstream. But the risk taker is immune to this. She is able to ignore all the prevalent conventions. The risk taker has a mind of her own. She is able to look beyond and assert her unique identity.

The risk taker recognizes that we are not involved in a dress rehearsal. This is our life, and we go around only once. To the risk taker, life would not be lived well were the risks not taken. The risks are viewed as necessary to having a quality of life that requires her to be the best that she can be.

Risks are an essential part of escaping the ordinary and developing as a unique personality. In short, if the risk taker has a motto, it would be: GO FOR IT. And the risk taker does go for it. Sometimes flinging caution to the winds. Sometimes filled with trepidation. But the risk taker recognizes that inaction leads only to mediocrity and she has no alternative except to defy common wisdom. "I'm not afraid of anybody," declares Becky Tedesco, a seasoned risk taker who has long since stopped being intimidated by even the most earnest of detractors.

There is enormous pressure in our society to persuade us to stay with the crowd, to avoid making waves. Unfortunately many of the unique aspects of a personality cannot be repressed in the comfortable mainstream of our society. So the woman who feels that her unique characteristics are being repressed has no alternative but to assert her independence. Any action taken to pursue the sound of her own private drummer entails risking the approval of those who hear a different music.

Incidentally, having taken risks in her life and become comfortable with her independence, the successful risk taker makes other small adjustments to enable her to be more forthright about her predilections. She dresses independently, arranges her schedule to fit her own natural rhythms, and frequently becomes more candid about her eccentricities.

"Conforming to what society thinks I should be like no longer interests me in the slightest," declares one successful entrepreneur. "I don't care who knows I'm a vegetarian, I do my best work at four in the morning, I meditate every day, and I'm nuts about my cats. I am who I am. People can take me or leave me. But I'm not going to try to be what I'm not. I can't even remember what normal people think and eat. It doesn't interest me in the slightest." This woman is not a misfit. She is an accomplished businesswoman who moves easily and successfully in traditional business circles. It is simply that she has a strong sense of self. This independence no doubt has contributed to her considerable success. Just as she has ceased to make unnecessary compromises to be successful in business, she asserts her personal predilections, too.

The independence of a risk taker frees her up to admit who she is without apologies. Says Becky Tedesco, "I'm an aggressive, bossy female who is terribly independent and have always been on some sort of path that led to upward mobility." The confidence she has gained with her long track record of success makes her even more independent—and independence fosters greater independence.

Indeed, the sense of accomplishment you can get from business success engenders independence. The successful risk taker is able to get a sense of identity and satisfaction that she cannot find anywhere else. This is the appeal of business to housewives, no matter how successful they have been at home. Notes Gale Lee Gilbert, who stayed at home as a traditional wife and mother for many years prior to starting her own limousine service, "I wanted to do something in my own right, to feel independent rather than

dependent." Like most risk takers, Gilbert cannot imagine returning to her previous less challenging life-style.

SCOLLARD'S LAW   Independence is addictive. Once you have
   achieved it, you cannot remember how it was that you were
   able to live without it. There's simply no going back.

SCOLLARD'S LAW   You can spot a woman who is her own
   woman across a crowded room.

Challenge. The independently minded risk taker knows that
there may be discouragement and adversity. Where the ordinary
person is deterred by a lack of encouragement, the risk taker has
her resolve strengthened by adversity.

A case in point is Christine Foster, who credits her current
success with discouragement that was given her. "I was told by
the head of the UCLA department that I'd have trouble later
getting a job because I am a woman. Well, I know the only reason
I'm in this business today and have been for the last twenty years
is because this son of a gun said I couldn't do it. I didn't really
know what I wanted to do, be a psychologist, a lawyer, but the
moment this son of a gun said I couldn't do it—that was it. I was
going to prove that I could."

A challenge can be almost irresistible to a risk taker. A challenge adds some excitement to achieving a goal. It adds suspense
and meaning to an endeavor.

Risk takers are often highly intelligent and capable people, to
whom many things come easily. A challenge adds interest. The
greatest pleasure may come not from achieving the goal but in
overcoming odds that critics said were insurmountable. "I did the
impossible" is often the biggest thrill a risk taker experiences.
Making money, building an empire, these things are often second-
ary in importance.

Inaction is abhorred by the risk taker, who is by nature an
activist. "The most important thing is not to be spinning your
wheels, but to be doing something that is challenging and fulfilling all the time," comments attorney Edith Fierst. "I am always
challenged and I am satisfied."

SCOLLARD'S LAW   The more difficult the task, the greater the thrill of completing it.

Excellence. Personal integrity is a highly valued trait among the most successful risk takers. The challenge is not only to achieve a certain goal but to do a better job than anybody else. The most successful risk takers have a competitive nature. But their most intense competition is with themselves. They find it far too easy to compare themselves with the average person around them. They have a strong internalized code of excellence and they judge themselves not by the outside world but by what they are capable of.

Patricia Harrison exemplifies this attitude. She says, "My big fear—and it may sound clichéd—is that I won't be the best. I want to be the best. That's me. I'm not in competition with anyone else. I want to keep learning. I'm afraid of ever doing things the same way because that's the way I've been doing them."

A West Coast–based executive agrees. "I think not being the best fuels me. It's very important for me to be the best at what I do. Even my physical exercise instructor laughs at me and calls me 'the animal.' I won't stop. I've got to be the best."

Risk takers are not averse to hard work. The work ethic is the other side of excellence. Change, which is the product of risk taking, almost always entails enormous effort. With each successful risk-taking experience comes a new goal. And the risk taker may have to expend enormous effort to achieve that goal.

In short, hard work comes with the territory. Successful risk takers know that you can affect the outcome of risk taking with sheer will and intense personal energy.

Comments television executive Lynn Loring, about how she achieved her success, "To be the best you have to work harder than the best. I'm regarded as truthful, honest, having enormous integrity, and being as tough as nails," Loring declares. Indeed, many of her associates refer to her as the Iron Butterfly.

Successful women typically find their work very satisfying. "I just love it," declares one. "I love working very much."

SCOLLARD'S LAW   Being the best is soul-satisfying.

Self-discipline. Of course, excellence is never achieved by accident. It is the result of self-discipline. Once you commit yourself to a risk, a change in the course of your life and career, then it is up to you to see it through. The initiative rests entirely on your shoulders. Your fate is up to you.

It is unlikely that any other person will prod you toward your goal. Chances are you must exercise stringent self-discipline, following a perhaps private agenda.

Implied in self-discipline, of course, is self-control. You don't have to be disciplined every day of your life. It is important to balance the commitment and the hard work with other aspects of living. "I can be the most disciplined person in the world and the most undisciplined in the world," says Lynn Loring. "I'm in total control of both."

SCOLLARD'S LAW You can call most successful risk takers at 8 A.M. on any workday and find them already at work.

HONOR

All the passion in the world offers little satisfaction in the absence of honor. The old cliché is true: It is in fact not whether you win or lose as much as it is how you play the game.

Risks are not undertaken in a vacuum. They occur in the context of society. There are rules. And some of the rules have to do with morality. The ideal is to take risks successfully and at the same time increase your pride in yourself and your capabilities. Moreover, you want to build a reputation among your peers that generates respect and esteem in them. Ideally you want to be known as playing fair and as being a generous, honest person. The esteem, admiration, and respect of those you deal with in the business world are important adjuncts to any success you accomplish. Indeed, in the unlikely instance that you should be put to a test, forced to choose between the satisfaction of achieving a certain business goal and ruining your good name, or losing all and enhancing your reputation, you might well opt for the latter. With the respect and esteem of your peers it would be easy to start over and take other risks that do not jeopardize the esteem your colleagues hold for you.

Success is not simply monetary. Ideally you can have it all, money and respect. But it is important as you chart your course of risk taking that you factor honor into the equation. No matter how successful a risk taker you are, if your reputation is sullied by mean-spiritedness or dishonesty, you are unlikely to achieve a sense of satisfaction or peace.

TEST YOUR HONOR

	YES	NO
1. My family's approval means a great deal to me.	——	——
2. If I have to choose between what I believe and what everyone tells me to do, I'll go with my own beliefs.	——	——
3. My parents don't care about my career.	——	——
4. I don't really care about getting recognition from my peers.	——	——
5. I believe that not rocking the boat will ensure that my colleagues will respect me.	——	——
6. It is important to consider what others think about us.	——	——
7. I love my family, but in order to be successful, I must neglect them for several years. It's worth it in the long run.	——	——
8. Once I'm successful, my problems will disappear.	——	——
9. Business is one thing. Taste and style are unrelated to it.	——	——
10. People don't care how you conduct your business as long as you make a lot of money.	——	——

	YES	NO

11. Your peers forget your bad moments once you make it to the top. ____ ____

12. Once you make a lot of money, your peers feel respect for you, even if they didn't on the way up. ____ ____

13. Make a lot of money any way you can, and then you can afford to clean up your act. ____ ____

14. If I feel with enough conviction that a certain direction is correct, I'll be able to persuade those around me of the wisdom of my course. ____ ____

15. My colleagues would want me to do what was best for me, for my self-esteem. ____ ____

16. Approval of my colleagues is important. ____ ____

17. I would never risk losing my father's approval, even if I felt worse about myself because of what I did to secure that approval. ____ ____

18. Style is more how you dress than what you do. ____ ____

19. Style is something you can't afford until after you are successful. ____ ____

SCORES:

Answer yes to 2, 3, 14.

Answer no to all others.

16–19 You are very honorable.

12–15 You need to trust in your own beliefs more.

10–14 You need to dare to be your own woman.

9 and below Study this book and try to develop a stronger sense of yourself.

It's difficult to write about self-esteem and respect because they are so personal and so relative. Also, the two may be in conflict. What makes you feel good about yourself may upset your colleagues and jeopardize the esteem in which you are held.

In these two subjects there are no absolutes, no hard criteria. What is important is that you factor these two aspects into your view of yourself and your risk taking.

Respect. The approval of those we love is always important to us. It is important to differentiate between those whose respect is important and those who make no difference in our lives.

"I've always been a pleaser," states ad agency chief Rebecca Tilton. "I like to make people proud of what I accomplish. When I make them proud and can share that success with them—that motivates me a lot."

Let's face it, there's nothing better than to have your parents sitting in the front row when you receive industry-wide recognition. Did you ever notice how presidents of the United States typically have their parents share the limelight at their inaugurations?

As you earn your reputation and gain the respect of your colleagues, there can be wonderful occasions when they gather solely for the purpose of honoring you. This recognition is soul-satisfying.

It's important, however, to distinguish between seeking respect and seeking approval. Seeking approval from everybody can be a deterrent to your success. It's a mistake to want everyone to approve of you.

But recognition is sweet. Gale Lee Gilbert says, "I'm elated when people around the country or world give me recognition and positive feedback. I have some friends who have put themselves out to be supportive. That's incredible. Because of it I've developed more confidence, spirit, vitality."

It's important, however, that you earn respect because you have taken a road that you feel is the right one. Should you pander for approval, you might find that you've lost essential parts of yourself in the process. Respect from others is sweet, but unless it results from actions you have taken that are compatible with and based on your self-respect, the glory will be empty.

Self-esteem. Even more important than the respect of the people you admire and love is that you know and love yourself. That self-respect is critical to deciding which risks to take. In the instance of Christine Foster, she looked inward when she decided to leave the convent and a vocation as a Catholic nun to enter the secular world instead. "What I learned most importantly was that I had to be true to myself. I couldn't lead my life caring what everybody else thought. Basically at a very young age I learned you've got to do what your heart tells you to do."

Changing your work objectives can alter your view of yourself. Certainly taking certain risks successfully significantly affects how you view yourself. One woman reports on how her relationship with herself benefited from having her own business. "The ability to make more choices in my life is a big reward. Getting in touch with myself is a big reward. The money was never a motivator for me. I can say it's nice. I'm motivated by challenges, problems, seeing all the parts fitting together like a wheel and making it more successful." She continues, "You need to know yourself very well and you have to question yourself and keep getting back in touch with yourself."

It's important that you keep a clear view of who you are, without being confused by money, titles, and other external values. One of the basic strengths you can develop is to keep a clear view of who the real interior you is and discover that you like that person. It doesn't happen without effort for some people. Says Lynn Loring, "I'm capable for the first time in my life of accepting myself for who I am. And liking that person for the most part."

Patricia Harrison, who has her own public relations and consulting firm in Washington, D.C., sees self-esteem as a central ingredient of success. "Know yourself and be yourself and then help others be themselves. To me that's really the true sense of power. Develop self-confidence. You have to be confident sometimes for other people. I have a core that is me that is of value. You can't always depend on external circumstances to validate you. People are not always going to pat you on the back. So you have to be able to provide yourself with that when you're not getting it from the outside."

There will be many moments in your risk-taking career when you find that there is no one to turn to but yourself. There will be times in the middle of the night when you are confronting your demons alone and making decisions. There will be moments of crisis where you have to make snap judgments. Trusting yourself will be an integral part of your risk-taking process. Your self-esteem will give you the confidence to go forward.

Frequently how you feel about yourself affects the decisions you make. Can you live with yourself if you fire an employee without notice? Can you live with yourself if you change your mind after you've shaken hands on a deal? Will you regret it if you permit an opportunity to go by?

SCOLLARD'S LAW If you don't have yourself, you don't have anything.

Quality of Life. Closely linked to respect and self-esteem is the quality of life that certain risks enable you to have. Once again, this is subjective and varies greatly from person to person. What is one woman's nirvana is another woman's hell.

What is important, again, is that you consider the quality of life that makes *you* happy. If you are shy and family oriented, you would take risks that enable you to live peacefully and have time to spend with your family. If you are an extrovert and single and love to work hard and want to be rich, you would consider an entirely different series of risks.

The point is that it's up to you.

Before you start down a road of calculated risks that will lead you to a destination, think about these things:

- Will you enjoy the journey? Life is short, and you must waste as little of it as possible.

- Will the ultimate outcome make you happy?

Remember that you are ultimately responsible for your life. You can be anything you want to be and you can have the kind of life you want to have. The choices are yours. Choose alternatives that make you happy.

One entrepreneur says she has discovered that the self-esteem her work provides is more important than money. She says, "Success means you know within yourself that you did something that makes you proud of yourself and happy. Now, I don't define that as money. I found out the hard way that that doesn't make you happy. You can buy everything you want to put your hands on, but that's not the thing that's going to make you happy."

Arna Vodenos, who is a twenty-nine-year-old entrepreneur, says she also values the quality of life she has created for herself. "I grow so much having my own business. Instead of having to go to the office and say, 'Can I get into this field?' I just do it. The freedom to grow is the greatest. Not only have I been able to gain financial independence, travel, meet people from all over the world, work with wonderfully creative, talented people, but it has helped me learn how to manage people, how to get the job done and how to meet deadlines."

Debbie McAteer says she has achieved a balance between her personal and professional life. "I bring personal work to the office and I bring work home. I'm married with a fifteen-month-old daughter and about to have another baby. It's hectic, but I'm so happy."

Another entrepreneur says she is propelled forward by the freedom to choose her destiny. "Also I love what I'm doing," she declares. "And my business has added enrichment to my life."

SCOLLARD'S LAW No matter how successful you become, there will always be problems.

SCOLLARD'S LAW The problems of success are highly preferable to the problems of failure.

Style. While you are weighing the options available and considering which risks are in fact worth the effort, one thing you might factor into your overall approach is your own personal style.

Webster's defines *style* as distinction and elegance of manner and bearing. Actually it's more than that, it's your own signature way of doing things. It's original. It's as personal as your signature.

It's a method, an approach to doing business. It is taste and "class." Once more, it is subjective, and how it appears is relative to who you are and which part of society you fit into. Moreover, it is regional. Texas style, California style, and New York style could not be more different on the surface, but the underpinnings of the three may be very similar. They may have to do with generosity, integrity, excellence, and graciousness.

Says one successful businesswoman, "I think the person who makes it is the person who sets his or her own style. She may be criticized for it. She may be admonished, envied. People may be jealous of her. It takes tons of courage to say, basically, 'Screw it.' This is who I am. I'm going around once. I have one life to live. And this is it."

Style has to do with how your quality of life is perceived from the outside. Often it has to do with attention to detail. It may be the follow-up call to congratulate a competitor who beat you out. It may be giving your entire staff a few days extra off with pay around Christmas. It may be honoring a handshake agreement despite a subsequent better offer. Style is your own individual imprint on your own organization and the business community around you. It affects your respect, your self-esteem, and becomes part of the quality of your life.

Certainly the easiest style to project is one of excellence and blue-chip service, product, follow-up, and attention. Being known as the best, the most elegant, is a lovely way to build a reputation.

SCOLLARD'S LAW   When in doubt, take the high road.

CREATIVITY

One of my pet peeves is people assuming that business and creativity are mutually exclusive. Recently, for example, after a lecture a woman stood in line to ask me what she considered to be a weighty and valid question.

"I'm creative, but I want to go into business," she said.

"Terrific. The best business people are very creative," I responded.

"No," she persisted. "I'm creative and that's the opposite of business. The only way I could go into business would be to ignore it and find a partner who would handle the business side."

"Are you a designer?"

"No, but I think creatively. I could never do business."

Actually, thinking creatively is the best way of approaching business. Creativity is not some special approach that is exclusive to the arts. Creativity is a way of looking at the world. It is a manner of synthesizing information and coming up with fresh solutions. It is a way of living. Although there are creative people, such as designers, who team up with marketing people to maximize their talents, most of the creative people I know have excellent business minds, and all of the successful business people I know have excellent creative skills.

One businesswoman realizes that she is fundamentally creative. "What makes me happy is creativity. Being able to think something up, figure out how to make it work, put it together, and see that it did work the way I wanted it to. To me, that is satisfaction. And satisfaction is success," she says. "My idea of happiness is to have an original idea that I can make work. And prove not only to myself but to other people that it does work."

Nowhere is creativity more useful than in risk taking. First of all, a fertile, creative mind perceives the needs and dares to dream of original solutions to meet those opportunities. For instance, Federal Express was a very creative idea. Perceiving the need in our accelerated society for overnight mail service was creative. Then the solution of processing all the mail through one city with aircraft solely dedicated to that purpose was an extremely clever solution.

You can use your creativity to find ways to motivate your employees, please your clients, and develop new businesses. It is important that when you are considering the risks you might take, you permit yourself to remove all of your prejudices and look at the world with fresh eyes. It is important to view yourself and your place in your world with imagination and an open mind. It is then that you will generate your best ideas and your most original solutions.

The day-to-day pressures and stresses of a business can limit your view and inhibit your creativity. To avoid this, you should structure your life to allow yourself to relax at some point in your day and create your best solutions. There are a variety of methods you can use. Some people meditate. Some merely instruct their secretaries to permit them fifteen uninterrupted minutes while they sit quietly. Others say they do their best thinking taking an early morning walk, playing with the children, or driving to work.

It doesn't matter when or how you achieve your most creative ideas. It differs from person to person. Investigate yourself, pinpoint your most creative moments, and structure your life so that you have access to these moments on a daily basis. Creative problem solving is one of the secrets of success.

SCOLLARD'S LAW   Creativity enhances every aspect of living.

SCOLLARD'S LAW   There is no one more creative than a successful entrepreneur.

TEST YOUR CREATIVITY

	YES	NO
1. Rules frustrate me.		
2. I would like to rewrite the rules.		
3. When someone tells me what the rules are, I figure there is a good reason and abide by them.		
4. I have a circle of friends I surround myself with. They are so terrific, there's really no reason to look for new ones.		
5. I am a fact gatherer. If I collect enough, I can make any decision accurately.		

	YES	NO

6. My friends tease me because I make mistakes they don't understand.

7. Being creative means one has a special talent, such as painting.

8. You are either born creative or you can forget the whole idea.

9. You should never let emotion interfere with reason.

10. The people who work with me are very attached to me.

11. I don't have a system for solving problems—the solutions come to me in different ways.

12. Daydreaming is silly, and I haven't done it for years.

13. I hate being the only one in the room who raises my hand when there are questions from the speaker.

14. My world is tidy. I don't like surprises.

15. My mate can read my mind.

16. I wish I could afford a decorator to design my living room.

17. Vegetarians are strange.

18. I am embarrassed if I go to a party wearing a cocktail dress and everyone else is wearing blue jeans.

19. Traveling with groups is far more educational.

20. I would like to take a trip to a strange place—alone.

SCORES:

Answer yes to 1, 2, 6, 10, 11, 20.

Answer no to all others.

15–20   You are a creative spirit.

12–15   You hold back too much. You should work on relating and trusting your instincts.

11 and below Team up with a free spirit. You'll be a great
team. You'll keep your partner's feet on the ground,
and your partner will teach you to look at life with
different eyes.

Curiosity. An open mind is a prerequisite of creativity. Cultivate a fresh perspective and learn everything you can. Often
things that seem extraneous or irrelevant turn out to be bits of
information that are keys to solving another totally unrelated
problem.

One effective way to open your eyes is to travel. Spending
time in Africa, Asia, or even Europe gives you an opportunity to
view our own American culture through different eyes. The basic
assumptions that we have here in America look ludicrous in Bhu-
tan or in the Hopi culture in Arizona. Don't be afraid to challenge
yourself.

You don't have to travel far to have your eyes opened. If you
live in suburbia, spend a weekend in the city and look at both
worlds without prejudice and with open eyes. In America totally
different cultures coexist only a few miles apart.

Curiosity takes commitment. A commitment to question the
most basic underpinnings, to consider alternatives. Curiosity
should be a commitment. A commitment to continually reassess
and reconsider our view of the world.

SCOLLARD'S LAW Curiosity didn't kill the cat. It helped her
develop her other eight lives.

Original Viewpoint. The result of a clear and fresh mental
attitude is a viewpoint that permits you to face risks in a new way.
Notes a seasoned risk taker, "I am creative. I like doing things the
way nobody else does them. That in itself makes me create
unusual things. It doesn't seem much of a challenge to me to do
something that's been done many times before. But it does seem
like a challenge to do something nobody else has done before."

Problem solving is one of the most creative acts in our society.
Whether it was Ben Franklin figuring out that a kite could tap
into electricity or Henry Ford deciding to mass-produce the auto-

mobile. The fresh viewpoint reveals solutions to risk takers that astound the rest of society.

SCOLLARD'S LAW Did you ever meet anyone who did handstands who was not enthusiastic about life? Even if it only means turning yourself upside down, looking at the world with fresh eyes can be a great business advantage.

Intuition. For once, we women have a substantial advantage in business. Our culture has encouraged us to develop our intuition. It is an important asset we bring to risk taking in our lives and businesses.

Ideally you gather all the objective information possible, listen to many different sources of advice, and then the moment of loneliness comes. The moment when you must make the decision about which direction to go. *You* have to face the decision alone. No one can make it for you.

Your intuition becomes an effective dimension of your decision making. Photographer Carol Highsmith declares, "Women are absolutely phenomenal. They are incredibly intuitive."

Anne Board, an executive at a large executive-recruitment company located on the East Coast, avers that women are doing well in her business *"because* they are very intuitive." Intuition is important in the personnel business, because it is a people business, and often instinct is the best guide in making judgments about people. A manufacturing executive admits that she relies on her intuition. "I have great gut instinct on projects and people," she says.

SCOLLARD'S LAW When in doubt, go with your gut feeling.

SCOLLARD'S LAW Chart the success of your gut. Keep a record of how accurate your gut feeling is.

Emotional Connections. Many creatively oriented risk takers forge deep bonds with other people. These relationships are formed at an instinctive visceral level and can prove stronger than the normal bonds.

Says TV producer Michael Linder, "There's a certain thing about sparking people's creativity. You become an icon, a lightning rod for attracting people's energies, and you draw it out of them and attract it to yourself. Then people start seeking you out because there's a magnetic force in you." Women often inspire these kind of relationships. Notes one executive, "I have an ability to establish very quickly important, deep emotional links with creative people. I understand their side of it."

There is an intensity shared by risk takers that attracts other people. They recognize the star quality of the risk taker. Her independence and intelligence stand out like a beacon in the night, attracting people who recognize her special character.

Because of her open mind and enhanced perspective, the successful risk taker often has deep understanding of the people she works with. This inspires deep loyalties. Indeed, the successful risk taker is frequently the Pied Piper to her employees and many of her peers.

SCOLLARD'S LAW   Risk takers are often charismatic. Their mental attitude makes them sexier and more irresistible than their physical characteristics justify.

CHARM

People skills are crucial in making any risk pay off. You have to cajole, persuade, enchant, entice, inspire, lead, divert, and understand people. Success in business and in risk taking is tied closely to your ability to read people correctly and make them do whatever it is that you need done to accomplish your goals.

Business is not for antisocial women. Business is by definition one of the most social acts there is. You constantly interact with people, and your success with them has much to do with the success of your risk taking.

Women have an advantage in this area in that we were taught to be charming. It is a cornerstone feminine grace, and one that serves us well in our risk taking.

Charm has been defined as the ability to persuade at least one other person that both of you are wonderful. You charm everyone you can. You charm your banker to back you, your clients to pay you up front, your suppliers to give you ninety days' credit, and your employees to persevere during the tough times.

People skills are the essence of risk taking in some businesses, such as personnel. "This business is totally dependent on your ability to manage people," notes Becky Tedesco, who runs her own temporary service.

Of course, the key ingredient of every kind of sales is charm. People buy you first and then consider your product or service. It's your charm that enhances whatever you are selling.

SCOLLARD'S LAW   Charm can make even the homeliest of women seem remarkably attractive.

TEST YOUR CHARM

	YES	NO
1. I am quick to let people know where I am coming from so that they can adapt to me.	___	___
2. I would just as soon listen as talk.	___	___
3. I am asked to dinner at least twice a week by friends.	___	___
4. When I go to a party of my friends, there is always a circle of them around me.	___	___
5. When I go to a party where I don't know anyone, I usually make a half dozen new contacts before I leave.	___	___
6. I would rather read a book than visit with friends.	___	___
7. Entertaining is a chore.	___	___
8. Laughter is one of my favorite pastimes.	___	___
9. People know to keep clear of me when I am under a deadline.	___	___
10. I tell jokes well.	___	___

	YES	NO

11. I keep a list of the birthdays of my associates. ___ ___

12. I keep a stack of greeting cards and small gifts on hand so that I am never caught unprepared for birthdays and anniversaries. ___ ___

13. I have been known to respond to a compliment by giving the admired object to the admirer. ___ ___

14. I prefer to meet people face to face when I want something from them. I figure my odds of getting what I want are better that way. ___ ___

15. People call me up just to tell me jokes. ___ ___

16. Sometimes I get a chuckle out of the most miserable of situations. ___ ___

17. I have been the president of at least one organization. ___ ___

18. I get frustrated because no one follows my advice—and I'm usually right. ___ ___

19. I project a much cooler exterior than I feel. ___ ___

20. I am an excellent cardplayer. ___ ___

21. I have to put the answering machine on my telephone to get a few moments' peace. ___ ___

22. When I am insecure, only my best friend knows. ___ ___

23. I know a great deal about the personal lives of my associates. I keep notes on the ones I only see rarely. ___ ___

24. Smiling comes easily to me. ___ ___

25. I feel shy when I first meet people. ___ ___

SCORES:

Answer no to   1, 6, 7, 9, 18, 25.

Answer yes to all others.

22–25 You are a natural-born charmer, and everyone knows it.

17–21 You can become charming without very much effort. Just pay more attention to the whims of your associates.

16 and below   Study this chapter. It will help you a great deal. Anyone can be charming. It is a skill that can be acquired with practice.

Receptiveness. An important ingredient of charm is the ability to pay attention to other people. To be attentive. To listen. It is flattering to them to be paid heed to. And the only way you can charm them is first to understand precisely what it would take to please them. It is important to assess the world from the point of view of the person you are dealing with. Says a successful communicator, "I think you really have to understand other people's motives, drives, needs, sorrows, and what they're going through." Then, and only then, can you respond efficiently to their needs.

Part of being receptive is listening carefully. Listening helps you with the art of relating to a client or any one you want to please. Women have an advantage in this area. Women are trained to listen.

Nancy Helmer, a commercial real estate agent, says, "I'm a good listener. And I'm a good negotiator." The two are closely related. It's much easier to come to an agreement on a deal when you've analyzed what it will take to please the other party. The negotiating subsequently is much more simple. When you've listened carefully before you've structured the deal, you are far more likely to have a satisfied customer. And, as everyone knows, the best deals are the ones in which both parties are satisfied.

SCOLLARD'S LAW   When you are listening, it's hard to make mistakes.

SCOLLARD'S LAW   Always listen before you speak.

Sense of Humor. A gentle wit, an ability to laugh at one's self, is a great asset in achieving success. It's an important part of dealing with people. "I try to avoid dealing with humorless people," says one successful risk taker. "Life is too short not to laugh."

A sense of humor can be an important ingredient in the success of tense negotiations. Adding the proper amount of levity at just the right time can take the edge off a difficult moment. It can divert everyone from stress and pressure and propel the meeting substantially forward.

Telling jokes is a good way to break the ice. It is also an excellent way to mask shyness. I, for one, am shy about picking up the telephone and calling people I don't know well. I've found that keeping up on the current jokes helps me deal with strangers on the phone. After I've told someone a couple of the latest jokes and they've chuckled, it's far easier for me to begin to talk to them about the reason for my phone call.

How do I find jokes? I have a very funny friend. She collects jokes and is always on top of the joke-of-the-day, whether it's related to politics, current events, or the weather. I check in with her a couple of times a week, and in ten minutes she's updated me on the hottest one-liners of the week.

Laughter is an important attribute, agrees producer Christine Dolan. "I maintain you have to have a good sense of humor because you can really shake up the boat a lot. Self-confidence and a sense of humor are really important characteristics if you want to be successful. You've got to be able to act silly." Dolan is right in grouping humor with confidence. It takes a lot of confidence to risk being funny and self-effacing.

SCOLLARD'S LAW   I've never met a stupid funny person.

Attention to Detail. Being charming entails remembering small, seemingly inconsequential things. It involves remembering the names of the children of your favorite clients, remembering wedding anniversaries, and that the dog was sick.

Attention to detail does not come naturally for most people. It is the result of shrewd observations and carefully kept notes.

When you have lunch with someone, listen carefully. As quickly as possible afterward, make notes of all the trivia your boss or banker or client discussed. Enter birthdays and anniversaries into a master log you keep for just such information.

People are enormously flattered when a business associate remembers small incidental aspects of their lives. They tend to be more favorably predisposed to such a person.

You might specialize in the kinds of details you remember. For instance, music. You might learn your banker's favorite music and from time to time send him or her a hard-to-find tape or record you know will please him or her. Or you might specialize in food and periodically send treats that are sure to please.

SCOLLARD'S LAW Some of the best deals are made because of absolutely inconsequential details having been attended to.

Persuasion. The point of being charming, besides embellishing the world you live in, is to get what you want. As we have discussed, you must *make* things happen to win at your risk taking. And one of the ways to make things happen is to persuade people to come around to your point of view. Being an excellent salesperson is integral to any business success. And the essence of sales is persuasion.

You must be able to demonstrate the merits of something. But having a superior product or idea is not enough. Regardless of the merits of your case, it is your ability at persuasion that will determine the success of your venture.

Being feminine can be a decided asset when you are being persuasive. Photographer Carol Highsmith believes so. "Women are very manipulative without seeming so," she says. "When I went to the American Institute of Architects, I looked like a little kid walking into the office saying, 'Hi. I want to do a book.' So they handed me this boiler-plate contract and said they needed it that afternoon. Three months later, when my lawyer got done with it, he said I had one of the highest royalty rates you could get." Highsmith thinks her low-key approach combined with her femininity caught the people she was negotiating with off guard.

SCOLLARD'S LAW Persuasion is most effective when it's friendly persuasion.

Leadership. "I've always been a leader," declares Nancy Helmer, a very successful realtor.

Not everyone is so lucky. Most leaders are not born. They are formed. Over time they develop certain aspects of themselves that generate confidence in people around them.

An important aspect of inspiring confidence is in giving people the idea that you really know what you are doing. Whether or not you do is not as important as the fact that everyone believes that you do.

If you are in a team situation, lead subtly. Persuade, cajole, and charm to such an extent that the other members are not ever aware they are being led. This subtle leadership avoids resentments and jealousies that might otherwise develop.

If you are the boss, appear humble to your employees. Praise them generously and frequently. Listen to their ideas. Put their ideas into action. Praise them copiously for this—maybe they'll have some more.

SCOLLARD'S LAW Most leaders are not born that way.

HOW DO YOU MEASURE UP?

Total the results of the four quizzes you have taken in this chapter. Your total score gives you an indication of how hard you need to work on developing your risk-taking abilities.

83 to 99: You are already a confident risk taker. You have the courage to take substantial risks. You have a track record of successful risk taking. You have a strong sense of your capabilities.

70 to 82: You are a proven risk taker but you need to develop a stronger sense of yourself. You can easily

train yourself to take risks more readily. You can also easily learn to take bigger risks.

60 to 69:   You still doubt yourself. You should practice taking small risks on a regular basis to demonstrate to yourself your ability. This book can help you recognize the successful risks you have taken and how to analyze future risks.

59 and under: You are timid. You fail to give yourself credit for the success you have already had as a risk taker. Study this book and develop a risk-taking schedule.

3   Priorities

RISKS LIE SOMEWHERE between our expectations of success and danger. When you risk, you walk a tightrope between a possible gain versus a possible loss. Obviously the acrobat who has practiced for years to learn her balancing act has a better chance of making it across the fine line than some notice who is unrehearsed.

Often an enormous—and the most difficult to analyze—risk is not to take a risk at all. This means that you do nothing. The problem with this is that while you are standing still, everything else in life is changing. Things will not be the same. Because even if you control your life and decide to keep it exactly as it is, the rest of life has gone ahead without you. So your circumstances will have changed whether you like it or not.

Some people make the mistake of thinking that if they don't take any conscious risk, if they "play it safe" and don't rock the boat, they will ultimately be secure because of their conservative approach. Some of these people kept their savings in savings bonds that paid 2 percent. The world changed. Their investments did not. They have been losing money for the past two decades.

The story of a woman in New York typifies the instance of taking few risks to assure a safe secure future. This woman twenty-three years ago started out in the broadcasting business, which was then exciting and golden. It had two decades of expansion and growth. During those two decades the woman kept the same job, never asked for raises, and figured that she was secure since she was never any problem. She was also making, after more than two decades of loyal work, far less than her colleagues—$26,000. Then the world changed. The broadcast industry's days of wine and roses came to an end and belt tightening has become commonplace in the industry as it routinely eliminates jobs to survive in its changed circumstances. After twenty-three years this woman was fired. She had minimal savings. And, after twenty-three years in one job in one company, her skills are virtually nontransferable to another company.

Says corporate executive Merry Clark, "Risk taking is associated with being an entrepreneur and having your own company. But you have to take risks to be successful as an employee in a company. There is a different way of taking risks in corporate life. On a project you are assigned, you have to get attention from the bosses to get a promotion. You have to be smart. Show your brains. Come up with new ideas. You've got to do something to be recognized. Women don't do this well."

Risk taking is the only way you can become successful. To gain much, you have to take risks. But this does not mean you must take a random gamble. To the contrary, you must do your homework. You can control many variables of a situation. You can choose your risks and manage them on your own terms.

Risk to Win is primarily about business risks, but the principles apply to your entire life. Learning how to win at risk taking is not just limited to business success, but to success in general. Getting married, having a baby, relocating, changing your life-style—all these acts entail substantial risks. Ideally the basic principles you learn to apply in business you will also apply to the rest of your life. The quality of it should be enhanced.

Life will only be comfortable for you if you learn to gain control of it. And choosing, planning, and timing your risks is an important part of managing your life.

There is always a reason why you take a risk. It is either because you need extra money, opportunity, challenge, or simply because a change seemed so natural, so effortless in the scheme of your life.

SCOLLARD'S LAW All risks entail change. Be prepared for things to become different.

Necessity. Frequently the motive that propels us forward, albeit reluctantly, is necessity. You need the money. You need the opportunity. You need the job. Necessity is indeed the mother of invention. There's no question that it prompts the shyest and most reluctant of us to go for goals that we might timidly have bypassed otherwise.

Kaye Lani Rae Rafko, Miss America of 1988, says necessity was what prompted her to compete. "It wasn't really my dream to be Miss America. I was so money hungry," she relates. "I just really wanted to be able to say that I paid for my college education, and Miss America was a way to do that—so I took advantage of it." She continues, "The only reason I began competing in the Miss America Pageant—and I began competing when I was seventeen in a local pageant in my hometown—was because they were offering a scholarship for school. That's what really interested me. I had been studying a variety of dance forms, including Hawaiian-Tahitian, and decided to do that for my talent. So I put on an older swimsuit I had. I used an old interview suit. And I wore my junior prom dress. And went out there and ended up winning and went on to Miss Michigan and placed second runner-up and won a fifteen-hundred-dollar scholarship and went directly to school. I was in nursing school at the time, and it was too costly for my parents to pay, and I had taken out a variety of student loans." She claims that she never expected to win. "When I made the top ten finalists, I prayed that they'd call my name. I prayed when they said fourth runner-up and third runner-up, and after they said first runner-up, I said, 'Well, thank you God for bringing me this far.' I had no idea I was going all the way. I was very surprised. Shocked. The first thought really was, 'My thirty thousand dollars! Now I can go back to school—my loan is paid off.' " Now she says she has paid off all her loans and has thirty-two thousand dollars to finance her through her master's degree.

It took a lot of guts for Rafko to enter a beauty competition. But necessity can be a fantastic motivator. "I've never considered myself beautiful," she admits. "I still don't."

Another woman recalls how she took a big risk because she felt she really needed a job in television to become what she wanted to be. She says, "I went to the station for an interview, and they asked me if I knew how to operate a TV camera. I didn't—but I quickly said I did. I figured I could learn before anybody would know otherwise. As it turned out, I got the job. On a Friday. I was to begin on Monday. That gave me the weekend. Immediately I raced over to the library and checked out some books instructing me on how to operate a camera," relates the spunky woman, who was living in Ohio at the time. "I studied all weekend. Then I went to a camera store and talked a salesman into letting me practice. By the time I reported to work on Monday, I really did know how to operate a camera."

Ironically this woman was never called upon to use her hastily acquired camera skills. However, the media skills she acquired in that job were the basis for founding her own successful public relations company.

Nancy H. Blanchet decided to interview for a job to be a stockbroker because she needed money to support five children. She wanted a job that permitted her to work around their school schedule. "I looked around for a job—but how many bank clerks are allowed to come in at ten and leave at two-thirty?" she recalls. "I heard about stock brokerage accidentally while riding in a car to a funeral. I told a joke, and one of the guys in the car laughed and laughed, and one of them said to me, 'My God, you're a natural-born stockbroker.' I asked, 'What's that, what do they do?' He said, 'Oh them, they don't do anything. They're on the golf course all day.' "

Blanchet was intrigued by the flexible hours, so she persisted. "Then I asked him if they made any money. And he said, 'It's a sin and a crime how much money they make.' I thought, That's my job! So I went down the next day and got it."

If Blanchet had not needed the money, who knows where she would be today. As it is, she is vice president at Smith Barney in Washington, D.C.

SCOLLARD'S LAW   Often we look back and bless necessity for spurring us on to accomplish things we would never have accomplished otherwise.

CHALLENGE

Sometimes the lure of a challenge is what entices women into taking risks they might not otherwise have taken. "I'm always proving that something can be done," says a woman who particularly delights in bucking the traditional female stereotypes men hold. Nancy Helmer says that the challenge was what lured her initially into commercial real estate brokerage in California. "The men I was interviewing with told me that women fail in this business and they were very discouraging and told me not to get into it. It was not only that I was a woman, but I was new to the area and didn't have any contacts either." With two strikes against her, they said, she hadn't a chance of success. Of course the adversity simply spurred her on to greater heights, causing her to dazzle her detractors with her success.

SCOLLARD'S LAW The greatest challenge is to compete against yourself—and win.

Listening to Your Inner Self. Sometimes you go against the face of reason and take risks in your life because it *feels* right. It becomes a moral decision. You take risks solely because it seems to be the right thing for you to do. A perfect example of a decision made for this reason was Christine Foster's decision in 1965 not to be a nun anymore. "It was very traumatic leaving the convent," she recalls. "It was kind of scary because I didn't know what I was going to do. When I left the convent, I came home and changed out of the habit, and I remember sitting upstairs on my bed. Of course I didn't know how to put clothes together or how to get dressed at that point, and I remember I sat on the bed and just cried and cried." But she harbored no regrets at any time. She felt instead a "deep sense that all is right. This is what I'm supposed to do. It was the most wonderful feeling in the world."

Frequently you simply arrive at the moment of truth where you realize that it's time to change things. It's time to make a move. This is what happened to Carol Highsmith and spurred her to make a dramatic career change from broadcasting executive to professional still photographer. "I had worked in broadcasting eighteen years and had worked the whole spectrum, served on various boards, and I just got fed up with corporate life and the corporate games. So, I started taking classes in photography to get my mind off what I was doing during the day." Highsmith started photography as a hobby, documenting renovations of old buildings in Washington, D.C., for six years, working nights and weekends. When she got her first big commission, she was ready to leave broadcasting. The move seemed natural and easy.

Sometimes, when we see that our circumstances or our view of the world is changing, we fight it. We should not. Rather we should seek to understand the changes in our circumstances and respond positively to them.

SCOLLARD'S LAW   Change is frequently for the better.

You're only young once. Because of the special opportunities available, young women should be encouraged to take many risks and try many different things. If you are in your twenties, you should take full advantage of your youth and take a wide variety of risks to learn about the world and yourself. In your early twenties there are no career mistakes—only learning opportunities. If you do not like a job or project, simply quit and try something else completely different. No one holds it against you.

Some very interesting careers develop because women had this attitude when they were young. I, for instance, now an entrepreneur, lecturer, and writer, started off with a variety of jobs in my late teens and early twenties. I worked in the following capacities:

Elementary schoolteacher	Discotheque manager
Receptionist	Paramedic
Cocktail hostess	Model
Secretary	Sculptor
Research assistant	

These work experiences were in five different states around the country, including New York and California. I leaped at every opportunity to travel around the world and explore as much of it as I could before I found a direction that seemed "right." I was able to support myself—albeit meagerly—until I finally found my first niche as a business writer, editor, and columnist. But what a great view of the world I had before I settled down to the business of being serious about my career.

When you open yourself up to experiencing different opportunities and discoveries, your career may end up on a faster track because of your broadened worldview than if you take the safe, "sure" route. Moreover, you are less afraid, because you have had so much experience getting different kinds of jobs.

Rebecca Tilton, who now, with a partner, has her own advertising agency, was, in her early twenties, a freelance special events coordinator in Denver. While organizing her own PR firm, she was working as a waitress when she met her current partner, waiting on his table. Her menial interim job was responsible for launching her current success.

You don't have to be a kid to explore a variety of different opportunities. You can do it at any age. Sally Marshall, now a television producer, entered her current career at age forty. She recalls, "When I first started in production, behind the camera, I had never done it. I showed up at the office because someone had the faith in me to say, 'I know you can cast this show. I know you can get these people.' I had never done anything in that area before and didn't know how to do it. So I showed up with an empty Rolodex and a saying, 'No one is more than three phone calls away.' I kept saying that for the first two shows. Now I have six Rolodexes—all jammed."

At any age, an open mind is your greatest asset. The ability to shift gears is a fundamental virtue also, providing you with opportunities to explore the world and enjoy your life. After all, the object is to have a rich and fulfilling life. Risk taking is the vehicle that opens the world for you.

SCOLLARD'S LAW Opportunity is not just for the very young. It's for anyone with a young attitude.

RISK–TAKING AS AN IMPORTANT PART OF SUCCESS

Before you make any decisions about risk taking, you must first have your priorities very much in place. You can design your life to fit your priorities and your own individual personality. Ask yourself questions such as these:

What kind of life do I want to lead?

How hard do I want to work?

Where do I want to work?

How much time do I want for leisure time?

Do I want my career to be the focal point of my life?

Do I want my husband and children to be the focal point of my life?

Do I want my children and career to be the focal point of my life?

Do I want my husband and career to be the focal point of my life?

Do I want it all—husband, children, and career?

Do I want to make a great deal of money?

How much stress can I handle?

Is creativity the most important gratification for me?

Am I people oriented?

Is travel important to me?

Do I want to work for anyone?

Do I want job security?

Where do I want to live?

What do I want to have accomplished by the time that I am seventy?

How many years do I want to work?

How much structure do I need to function optimally in my work?

Obviously, if you are a family-oriented introvert, you are going to make different choices from an unmarried extrovert workaholic. It is important that you examine yourself and be honest about what makes you happy.

When I talk to women, they always tell me they want to be happy, but it is surprising how many of them have not isolated the factors that are required to make them happy.

Happiness is usually very simple, but it differs for many people. One woman says the following is her recipe for happiness:

1. Do something with your life that you truly enjoy. Find out what you like and do it.

2. Love someone. If not some *one*, then a pet.

3. Always have something to look forward to. Even if it's dinner with friends on Saturday night. Always have plans.

Break down for yourself what makes you happy—and what makes you unhappy. Take a sheet of paper and divide it in two columns. On one side list what makes you happy and on the other side list things you do not like.

HAPPY	UNHAPPY
Flexible hours	Structured work
Being my own boss	Bureaucracy
Lots of small vacations	Working with disagreeable people
Husband	Cold and wet or hot and humid climates
Money	Worrying about paying the bills
Problem solving	
Challenges	

With only a short list you can find out a great deal about what makes you happy. The person who put together this list is obviously only going to be happy living in a moderate climate, running her own business—probably a small one, since she dislikes bureaucracy—in an industry that is both lucrative and seasonal so that she can take time off. She needs a good assistant to back her up, since she values flexible hours and free time.

Keeping sight of your priorities must be a priority in itself. Sometimes it's easy to lose your way and forget who you are. Says

Rebecca Tilton, whose Denver agency is very successful, "I lost touch with who I was for a while. A lot of times we can get caught up in this whirlwind of power and position and titles. And we forget who we really are and forget to stand up for those things."

When you write down your happinesses and miseries, keep the list. Tuck it away and refer to it periodically. The bottom line should always be that you are taking risks that enhance your chances of being completely happy. We only go through this life once. It is important that we reap the greatest happiness out of every day.

SCOLLARD'S LAW   As you grow, you may find that some of the things you thought would make you happy don't. As soon as you discover this, revise your priorities.

Money. Making a lot of money is a primary objective for many people. For one thing, money is the currency by which our society confers a certain amount of respect and recognition. If you make a lot of money, the rationale goes, you must be good at something. Moreover, money buys a lot of things that may be of value to you. Homes, car, travel, jewelry: Money supplies many opportunities.

One woman says her priority is "to be financially successful, where people know me and the company and feel the name is something substantial and solid in the industry." Obviously, to her, money and respect go hand in hand.

Money is a popular priority. But sometimes people become so interested in making it that they lose sight of their other priorities. It is important to remain in touch with all of your values, to have a balanced view of the things in life that are important to you.

Money may be a priority for a while—until you've earned enough. A woman who runs a highly profitable business in Houston says that money is a priority for her for the next few years. She's working seven days a week, eighteen hours a day, to build a small empire. When she's thirty-five, she declares, she intends to go into early retirement and develop a different set of priorities. Then she intends to get married and make her family life a priority, living off the fortune she's accumulating now. "Nobody in their right mind would marry me while I'm working this hard," she says. "But in a few years I'm going to buy a big boat and put in a computer bank on the boat and run the business from there and completely change my life."

SCOLLARD'S LAW Priorities are personal. Don't let anyone tell you what you *ought* to value. Go for the things that you know make you happy.

Flexibility. When you have children, flexibility becomes a central priority in your work. The only way you can juggle the demands of your work with the demands of motherhood is to have work that allows for you to manage your time to take care of both.

This can be difficult if you have a job working in corporate America. Corporate America was designed for men. And men had wives who took care of the children. Since *we* are the wives, it can be difficult. When you work in corporate America, you may limit the hours you put in at the office in order to rush home and be with the children. Says Sally Marshall, "My time with my kids is very important, at the risk of having people say, 'You're going home at six?' And I say yes. Because if I can't get done what I need to get done between nine and six, I'm not doing a good job. It's interesting that I've been able to change a lot of people's attitudes about getting their work done and getting it done in those hours."

Nancy H. Blanchet, as we have noted, chose her job as a stockbroker because it had flexible hours and she wanted to spend time with her five children. They were clearly her first priority. "I decided I would make as much money as I could with the time left over from being an excellent mother. And when I was first hired, I told my boss that I had a terribly important job—motherhood—and I would work as hard as possible for him when I had time. He thought this was a scream. It took him two years to realize that it was true in my mind that my professional job came second to my job at home." And Blanchet considers her "job" as a parent to have been more challenging than any job she tackled outside of the home. "If I had my choice, I would never have left home at all. I didn't want to go out to work. Any of my eleven jobs have been far less interesting than being a parent. Far less challenging. Required less humor, less intelligence."

Some sales jobs, such as the stockbroker's job Blanchet works at, permit you to be flexible and plan your life around your children. There are other corporate positions that are also tolerant of women's responsibilities to their children. If you work in one that takes a hard line, change jobs. Move to one that recognizes that you can be incredibly productive and have a family, too.

What many women are choosing to do to juggle their priorities is to leave corporate America completely and start their own businesses. They become the boss. They write the rules. Half of all the businesses founded today are started by women. The flexibility that you have when you're in charge permits you to utilize your professional skills at the same time that you're being attentive to your family. You can take your work to the nursery or the nursery to the office. It's up to you.

One woman who has her own real estate firm in New Jersey takes off the entire month of August every year to spend the time at the beach with her teenage sons. She says she doesn't care that August is a lucrative month in her real estate market. Spending time with her sons is a greater priority. She is taking advantage of the freedom you can have when you're in charge. Georgette Klinger, who heads up a chain of full-service beauty salons bearing her name, arranged for her daughter, Kathryn, to play in her salon after school. It was only natural for Kathryn to come officially into her mother's business when she grew up. She knew the creams and treatment products the way a lot of little girls know their dolls. The younger Klinger is now president of the company.

A business of your own can be a way of keeping the family unit together. You can have your children work in the business after school and in the summers. Instead of separating family units, business can be a vehicle for keeping it together.

Because of the advantages of entrepreneurship, some women who work in corporate America are delaying having children until they can move out and start their own businesses. Says one woman, "I would never ever consider having a child while I was working for someone else. But I'm thirty-four and now prepared to have a child because I've become self-employed. I picture myself having a lot of kids and working out of my home and being self-employed. It'll be a good life."

SCOLLARD'S LAW You can have children and a career, too. But it requires creativity to really pull it off.

Family Contact. If you do not have the flexibility that you would like in your work environment, you can still discreetly maintain contact with your children. One woman has her son and daughter check in as soon as they get home from school. Her staff know that the children are expected to call every day—but her boss doesn't. The woman discusses the children's homework with them and gives them instructions for dinner preparation. Moreover, the children check with her for permission to visit friends. "I don't know how women were able to work and have children before the invention of the telephone," comments the woman.

Attorney Dona Kahn says the telephone is an important link for her, too. "I always made sure I was at the phone every day at four o'clock when they came home from school. I would have my secretary interrupt me at a meeting and say, 'The White House is calling,' or 'The governor is calling,' or someone else important because I wanted my kids to be able to say to me what they wanted to say to me when they got home from school and not wait a couple of hours."

SCOLLARD'S LAW A generation of latchkey children has grown up, and they've turned out exceptionally well.

Husband. The man in your life may be a very important priority. It is possible to be a workaholic and stay married—if you're married to another workaholic who is as wrapped up in his risk taking as you are. But conflict usually arises when one of you is completely spellbound by your work and the other has leisure time and wants to play. If you love the man in your life, you have to be sensitive to his expectations when you are making commitments to your work.

There is no reason to apologize if your career decisions are substantially influenced by attachment to a man in your life, particularly if the relationship is more rewarding than your work. Chapter 8 discusses at length how risk takers are able to simultaneously sustain romantic relationships.

SCOLLARD'S LAW There's no opportunity I wouldn't turn down if it seriously jeopardized my relationship with the man in my life. Opportunities are plentiful. Soul mates are not.

Recognition. One of the gratifying aspects of success to some people is having people recognize what they've accomplished.

If you've accomplished what people said could not be done, there is no reason why you shouldn't be proud. You deserve a pat on the back. A former housewife says that one of her goals was to have her family "realize there were things I could do and wanted to do. I had become a fixture around the house. One of the reasons I built this business was to prove that point."

If recognition is important to you, go after it. Hire a public relations person to get the story of your success out before the public. Join organizations that will appreciate just what you have accomplished. Be visible. Understand that some people are embarrassed by recognition. Don't be embarrassed because you're not.

SCOLLARD'S LAW There can be great satisfaction in having people recognize that you did it—and you did it all your way.

"I Want It All." Women who want it all are very busy people. Children, husbands, careers, money, recognition, creativity— they go for it. It's tough, but it's possible. Not everyone can do it. But some people can. Maybe you're one of those who can.

What it probably means is that you are better at some things at certain times in your life than you are at others. For instance, you can probably handle a husband and a career. But when children come into the picture, priorities have to be reevaluated. You may decide to redirect your career to give you some breathing room or to start your own business.

If you want it all, you will have to make compromises. There will be nights when you are less than a perfect wife—definitely not seductive. There will be times when you feel guilty about not being there for your children. There will be contracts you blow in your business because there were other things on your mind. And there will be long periods where you leave absolutely no time for yourself.

If you want it all, you have to be resourceful and adaptive. The most creative aspect of your life is juggling your priorities. They will change on a daily—and sometimes hourly—basis. You have to be flexible, quick on your feet, and really dedicated to having it all.

If you want it all, you also have to have a sense of humor. And your mate will need one, too. And the children will learn it from the two of you. And you will have to build the family unit so that it operates as a team. You and your family will have to pull together much as though you were in a sailing competition, first on one side and then, as you tack into the wind, all shifting quickly to the other side.

Going for it all is not for everyone. Some people have difficulty balancing their risk taking with a personal life, not to mention the added stress of children and great ambition. Going for it all requires compromises and less-than-perfect performances in different areas at different times.

Once again, it's a matter of your priorities. Perhaps you prefer to have it all—but sequentially. There are no rules. It's up to you to decide how to live your life so that it will make you happy.

SCOLLARD'S LAW   Be careful what you wish for because your wishes may come true.

SACRIFICES

Success frequently requires sacrifice. What you sacrifice is up to you. It's a personal judgment based on how you feel about yourself, what your priorities are, and what makes you happy. Sacrifices are not forced. They are a matter of choice.

Sacrifices are very real. There's nothing phony about them. You simply commit yourself to whatever your priorities are and forgo other things.

The sacrifices are different from the ones men have to make. Because they have us, as wives, they have long been able to have it all—marriage, children, career. For women, it's different. We have husbands. And we have a hard time having it all. Very often we decide it's too much. And we choose. The choices are not fun, because we're giving up parts of ourselves and aspects of our lives that we once thought essential.

Children. One of the most common sacrifices is one that was unthinkable a generation ago: forgoing having children. This is a sacrifice that most men have never had to consider. But since we bear the children and are typically left to be economically responsible for them, as well as culturally and socially, they can be perceived more as a burden than a blessing. Some of the most interesting women in our culture have decided not to have them. That leaves them time for everything else, the men in their lives, risk taking, friends, and their selves. Children take an enormous commitment and effort. These women figure that if they forgo having children, they can manage everything else.

Some women suffer through their decision and harbor small regrets forever. Other women are able to make the choice more blithely. "We never wanted children," explains one woman. "They were never a priority." "Ultimately having no children is a sacrifice, though I don't feel badly about it," comments another.

But other women feel that they would have liked to have had children but didn't. Says a woman who founded a very successful business with her husband, "I feel we have sacrificed having children. We've been so busy. I woke up one day and found myself too old to have a kid. There are times I wish I had children. We were too busy and we got selfish. You always figure you can have a child later on, and then you wake up one day, and bingo—it's too late."

If you do have children, juggling them with your career is a problem, unless you forgo your career for a few years. Your priorities are constantly shifting, and feeling guilty about neglecting your children is commonplace.

A woman who stopped being a full-time housewife and mother to pursue a stellar career in television says she regrets changing the rules for her son. "My son's life was turned upside down. He suddenly had a mother he hadn't bargained for. He used to have a mother who was always home and ready to help with homework. Then suddenly, when he's twelve years old, I'm not there for him. I have enormous guilt for what I did to him, which I'll have forever." She also feels guilty about the lack of time she has for her eleven-year-old daughter. "She only sees her mom on weekends. That's not how you're supposed to raise children."

However, other women have been able to balance their careers with their childbearing much more happily. For instance, Patricia Harrison had three children, ages twelve, seven, and five, when she founded her own business. "There's no way, I believe, of saying there's quality time and quantity time. There's just time. All a kid knows is you're either there or you're not there. So it's a conflict, and you almost have to ask the children how good a job you did. I have no idea. One thing I always tried to do was let them know why I was doing what I was doing and how it would benefit them. So I didn't feel I was off on my own creating this business. I thought that all of us were part of it." Harrison worked hard to engender the sense of team spirit with her children. "Just simple things, like bringing my kids to the office so that they could physically see where I was. Any time they called, that was the priority call, all the time. So they knew they could get through. They still do that—I'll be 110 years old and they'll still be calling me at three o'clock in the afternoon."

Harrison also rewarded her children so that they could see benefits to her working. Once a week they had dinner out together, and the children could pick the restaurants. She says her children saw her company as a "financial benefit." She believes that part of their acceptance of her building her company had to do with the attitude she presented to them. "I think it's how you present information to people that affects how they interpret whether it's good news or bad news." She feels that if her guilt prompted her to apologize to them, it would be negative.

So, you see, a great deal about how you feel about working and having children has to do with you. Your personality. Your attitude. Some women are simply better equipped to handle the tug-of-war that results from wanting to give the most of yourself in two or three different areas.

You must be honest with yourself about how well you can handle the situation of business risk taking and childrearing. The solution you arrive at will be a personal one. Don't let anyone intimidate you into doing what seems best for you. It's a very personal decision.

SCOLLARD'S LAW What makes one woman guilty may not affect another woman.

SCOLLARD'S LAW A good national child-care system would simplify things enormously for women.

Marriage. Frequently women delay marriage until it is a convenient moment in their careers to devote the time necessary to have a good relationship. Some women feel it isn't worth it. Says a woman who opted for singlehood, "I could not give the effort and time required. I looked at marriage and my career and decided I'm going to pursue the career. It seemed more sensible for me, and I don't regret it."

Once again, sacrificing marriage is something women are more likely to do than men. Because we marry husbands. And they get wives. Husbands require a great deal more care and feeding. When a man is without a wife, he has a handicap. When a woman is without a husband, she has fewer demands on her time.

The self-realization that occurs in successful risk taking is often at odds with a woman's role in her marriage. And frequently, as is discussed at length in chapter 8, divorce ensues.

One informal observation, based on my interviews for this and other books: More entrepreneurs tend to be happily married than are executive women. Perhaps the flexibility of being your own boss is more conducive to allowing the time for marriage.

SCOLLARD'S LAW   The happiest people balance their business lives with a full and round personal life—not necessarily marriage, but a gratifying life away from their work.

Other Things. One of the first things that women sacrifice is time for themselves. Treat yourself with the same care that you do a privileged client. Schedule time for yourself in your daily agenda.

We also sacrifice the traditional duties that our mothers used to perform—baking cakes from scratch, making quilts and Christmas decorations. Don't blithely let go of all these things. Keep the ones that are important to you. Call it a hobby. It's healthy to have several hobbies, whether it is gardening, skiing, walking, or birdwatching. And it's interesting how once something becomes a priority, you can find some time in your life for it.

SCOLLARD'S LAW   If you want something done, ask a busy person.

REWARDS

There are benefits. Obviously, women wouldn't make the sacrifices they do if there were not gratifying aspects to their lives. One entrepreneur says she luxuriates in the sense of freedom. "This is the first time I feel in control of my life. That I can direct my destiny. To me that's a wonderful feeling."

Although money is an objective in your risk taking, it usually isn't money that you talk about when you talk about the satisfaction. Says Sally Marshall, "My success is not so much in financial gain as that I made a huge career change at age forty and feel now, at age forty-six, that I'm still getting ready to peak. I have a lot to look forward to."

Says another woman, "I feel more self-confidence and I'm happy. What I try to do is look for the personal fulfillment within my job. Seeing people blossom under my care—these things are very important to me, and to that extent I feel very personally fulfilled."

Another successful entrepreneur declares, "I get a tremendous amount of satisfaction working. I meet incredibly wonderful people who are supportive. I've opened up a whole new vista I never would have imagined if I had never started my own business."

Part of the reward is the sense of satisfaction that you've taken risks and changed your life and succeeded. To outsiders you may look lucky, but you have no doubt learned that you make your own luck. Your accomplishments become a part of you that no one can take away.

Says a happy risk taker, "I live my life in a way that makes me happy today and also with an eye toward when I'm ninety years old. When I reach that age, I want to be satisfied that I did the most I could do, as best I could. I don't want to miss anything."

SCOLLARD'S LAW   Life is long enough to do much more than we expected.

4

How to Analyze
Your Risks

RISK TAKING for its own sake is fool-
ish. There is a big difference in the kinds of risks you encounter.
This chapter gives you tools to address whatever risks you have
in your life so that you can choose the course of action most likely
to succeed. Here we will examine the methods that investment
advisers use to quantify their risks. We will observe what the pros
do—the bookmakers who calculate the odds in sports. And we
will analyze two different case histories.

Until you are a seasoned risk taker, risks may be a bit daunting.
But the techniques we discuss will help you become expert at
assessing situations and making decisions. Taking risks constructively will enhance your life. Says one entrepreneur, "Risk yields
greater return on your investment, whether it's money, love, or
trying to climb the highest mountain."

SCOLLARD'S LAW   It's exhilarating to risk and win.

HOW WALL STREET
DEALS WITH RISK

Our lives are more important than our financial investments. But
frequently we devote long hours to analyzing our investment
risks and then take a spur-of-the-moment risk in other aspects of
our lives—quitting a job, getting pregnant, starting a new business.

We can learn from investigating the kinds of analysis investment experts use to limit the size of their risks in portfolio management. Observes Steven C. Leuthold, whose Minneapolis-based company advises money managers, "To me, risk is what chance you have of losing money."

There is no magic way of absolutely calculating your chances of winning—or losing. The attempt to do so occupies thousands of hours on Wall Street every day. Basically investment advisers use history and try to project from it. Leuthold gives an example of how they think: "The past odds have been that if you bought a company at fifteen times earnings, you would make money in three out of four years. And that if you bought a company at twenty times earnings, you would make money in one out of four years." So obviously your risk is less if you buy the company at fifteen times earnings.

An important factor in investment decisions is whether or not the risk of buying stocks is worth it. For instance, the least risky investment is U.S. bonds. If they are paying 9 percent, that is a fairly riskless rate of return. A bond is a contract to get your money back, and the deal is that unless the U.S. government defaults, you will be paid. If risk is ranked 1 to 100, with 100 being the safest, U.S. bonds are the safest, according to most investment advisers.

If you want to make more than 9 percent on your money, you will have to take a greater risk. "You'd have to have a good case to justify owning stock that is just part of a company when the U.S. government is guaranteeing 9 percent," notes Leuthold. So you would evaluate stocks and the amount of risk and the amount of return—based on history—and see whether the risk is justified.

Shannon Clyne, a senior vice president and money manager at Bank of America in California, spends a great deal of time analyzing the volatility of various types of investment and then studying the market itself. Certain types of investment perform differently in different parts of an economic cycle. He breaks the cycle down in four phases. And he knows which investments perform best in which phase.

But the hard part is figuring out when we are moving from one phase to the next. And it's impossible to predict with any certainty. So Clyne, like everyone in the investment game, is reduced to intelligent guessing.

Clyne studies history at great length and tries to make as informed a decision as possible. But there are no guarantees when you are projecting the future based on past performances. Unfortunately the stock market has none of the reliability of the sun rising every day.

Richard Russell is another very smart student of the economy and market. He writes a highly regarded newsletter, the *Dow Theory Letter*, and he says, "The easiest way to pick a stock is to look at the credit rating. It tells you how solvent the company is." But the most important aspect he considers is the main trend of the market. He advises, "If it's a bear market, don't buy. If it's a bull market, buy the best and safest stocks you can find."

The trick—and there is always a fundamental guess in the investment game—is to know how the market is going. "Most of my work is spent studying the trend of the market," says Russell, who describes his personal orientation as "very conservative." To succeed in the market, he advises, "You have to have an intelligent strategy and stay with it." For instance, when he looks for a stock to buy, he opts for one that is outperforming the market. It's only common sense. "It's the same when I want to buy a house. Then I buy in an area that's doing better than anyplace else," he explains.

Ed Sezna, an investment expert at Sezna Floyd and Hamanaka in Los Angeles, frankly states that he believes that the best stock analysis is subjective: "I don't believe anyone can quantify risks on a percentage scale. There's nothing quantifiable," he says. If you assume anything insured by the U.S. government is one hundred on a relative scale, the values of other investments vary from investor to investor. Says Sezna, "An oil and gas investment might be a thirty to me. But to a geologist who knows about those things, it might be ranked differently."

Summary. Let's analyze what these investment experts have told us and see what we can learn from their rigorous and carefully researched techniques in order to apply them to the risks in our lives.

1. We cannot predict the future. But we can study history, analyze it carefully, and use it as a basis for the future. Some things are historically riskier than others. We can isolate those factors.
2. The greater your risk, the greater your up-side—and down-side—potential.
3. Look at the safest alternative. Are the returns you can expect from taking risks worth it?
4. Timing is critical. A risk that would be relatively safe in some circumstances would be foolhardy in others. Learn the difference. Be alert to the economy you are operating in.
5. Develop a personal life strategy and make your decisions within that context. Keep a clear view of your priorities.
6. Know your objectives. Keep them in mind when you evaluate risks.
7. Ultimately, all risk taking is a judgment call. If you do your homework, your call will be better.
8. It takes lots of homework. Even the experts spend most of their time studying.

We will use these important points when we are studying case histories. But first let's see how the bookmakers analyze odds.

SCOLLARD'S LAW   There is no shortcut to risk analysis.

SCOLLARD'S LAW   Be as analytical about your life's risks as you are about your investments.

HOW THE BOOKMAKERS VIEW RISK

When you go to the racetrack, you see some evidence of efficient risk evaluation. Some horses are ranked with odds of 10 to 1. That means the oddsmaker is willing to give you $10 for any $1 you bet on the horse winning. That means that of the total amount of money bet, ten times as much as been wagered against that horse as has been bet for it.

But if the odds are 2 to 1, it's probably a much better horse. And much more likely to win that race. The oddsmaker has tallied up the dollars bet and found that twice as much money has been bet on the horse losing as on winning.

What the oddsmaker at the horse track has done is quantify the mood of the money that is being bet. If you are cautious, you will take the one that has odds of 2 to 1. At least you have a 50 percent chance of winning. You make less, but your chances are far better than if you take the 10-to-1 horse. On the other hand, the 10-to-1 horse would pay five times more money if it won. The greater your risk, the greater your possible reward.

Generally, the mood of the money reflects some very serious research of the sport and of the particular event, be it a race or a game. Big-time bettors often subscribe to the services of professional pundits in Las Vegas. They are full-time students of the sport they advise on and for a fee will share their expertise. For instance, they attempt to quantify the risks in a football competition. They give you a point spread—the number of points by which they believe one team will beat another. Their thinking might go like this:

TEAM A

Quarterback is better—1 point
Offensive line is better—1 point
Defensive line is tougher—1 point
Coach is better—1 point
Desire to win is great—1 point
They're the home team and the town loves them—1 point

So, Team A would be the 6-point favorite over Team B.

There's nothing scientific about this. It's all based on homework. It has to do with history and judgment calls on the part of the bookmakers. Intuition plays a big part in the judgment call. They might feel the quarterback is better than he's looked because he hasn't had the proper backup in the last two games. Or they may expect the team to come to life and so gave them a point on desire.

The pundits do their homework. They know the injuries each team has and how the players are likely to perform. They know how good the replacement is if the quarterback is out with an injury. They know who is in the lineup for the game, who is likely to start.

There are variables even the most thorough student cannot determine. Misplays, interceptions, fumbles—these no one can foretell. It's just the same as the stock market, where no one can predict a corporate takeover or a bomb going off in an oil field or a serious drought.

Summary. There's much to be learned from the betting community.

1. Be creative and thorough in your fact finding.
2. Use your best judgment after you've studied the fact to assign mathematical probabilities.
3. Use your intuition—one of women's greatest assets.

SCOLLARD'S LAW Your bookie is probably more realistic about risk taking than you are.

COMBINING RISKS:
The 10 Factor

Bookmakers and stock market gurus have one tremendous advantage over us when it comes to evaluating risks: It's their business. It's what they do for a living, what they've done for years. When we sit down to evaluate our risks, we have three major disadvantages:

- We don't have access to the research and we won't do as much homework.

- We are more emotional about the judgment and see the situation less clearly. It is, after all, ourselves that we are risking.

- We don't isolate the risks.

The last of the above-mentioned disadvantages is the most serious. If you take one risk at a time and analyze it, you are in a better position to make the right decisions. You need to space out your risks to be able to see the ramifications clearly. Otherwise you run the chance of multiplying the likelihood of failure. Several risks taken at one time have a snowballing effect. Whenever you combine your risks, you multiply the odds against your success by ten times—the 10 Factor.

For instance, a thirty-eight-year-old woman who had believed she could not have children recently discovered she was pregnant. Single, but pregnant. She was overjoyed and thrilled at the opportunity to risk having a child. But she immediately added another risk to the situation. She married the man who made her pregnant. It was a spur-of-the-moment decision, and to others it seems an unstable, unsuitable match.

The 10 Factor comes into the marriage. The risk of the marriage—any marriage—surviving under the best of circumstances is 1 out of 2. But in the presence of another major decision—the pregnancy—the odds against the marriage risk multiply by the 10 Factor. That means her chance of the marriage succeeding is now only 1 out of 20.

To take risks and win takes careful preparation. The negative consequences of bunching your risks up don't add the odds up against the outcome, they *multiply* them. To take risks successfully, space them out.

Give yourself time so that you can make your best effort in order for your risk to win.

Let us consider what happens if you take three risks at once. For instance, if you were to simultaneously get a divorce, relocate, and change your career—three big risks—the odds of your succeeding deteriorate. Ideally you would deal with the risk you cannot control and delay making the other decisions. Perhaps your divorce is the situation you cannot control. Perhaps your husband ran off with another woman and you have no recourse but to divorce. But you can control the timing of the other two risks. You can wait six months or a year before you undertake any voluntary changes in your life.

If you take all three risks at once, examine what happens with the 10 Factor introduced not once but twice. You are divorcing and you relocate. The odds of your being happy in another city under the best of circumstances would have been just about even. But combined with the divorce, they become 1 out of 10—the 10 Factor.

The odds against the third risk become even worse. Say you are starting a new business at the same time. Under the best of circumstances, let's say your odds of succeeding were 1 in 4. Combined with the divorce, it becomes 1 in 40. Combined with both the relocation *and* the divorce, the 10 Factor is at work twice, and the chance of success in your new business becomes 1 in 400.

Now, 1 in 400 is not impossible, but it makes life far more difficult. Why do that to yourself? Simplify your life. Avoid the 10 Factor whenever you can. Space your risks out so that you can give them the attention necessary to make the odds in your favor.

When you are confronted with a risk you have little control over, such as getting divorced or getting fired, put as much of the rest of your life on hold as possible. Give yourself six months to a year before you undertake any voluntary risks. Give yourself time to evaluate, do your homework, and develop a realistic perspective.

Pace your life as much as you can. Some things you cannot control. But many risks you can. Pace the timing so that you can give the risks you can control the kind of attention that engenders successful risk taking.

When you combine your risks, you muddy the water. And your prospects for success become much less.

SCOLLARD'S LAW The successful gambler lives by the odds. Don't stack the odds against yourself.

RISK–TAKING CASE HISTORY

You are considering opening a restaurant. How do you decide if it is a good idea? Let's apply what we've learned from the investment gurus and bookies to analyze the risk.

Before you can have an opinion of any kind about the merits of the project, you must do your homework. Historically what are the odds for survival of a restaurant in general? Is your restaurant a special situation? Are its odds better or worse? Are the odds for survival 1 in 4? 1 in 10? Is the risk worth it? Would you be better investing in something else?

Borrowing from the bookies, rank these variables from 1 to 10, 10 being perfect. But before you rank these variables, you would have to extensively research the business, your particular location, the projected menu, and the competition.

Is the economy right for your restaurant? ____
How intense is the competition? ____
How are the other restaurants doing? ____
Is the time right for another one? ____
Is location important? ____
Can you get the ideal location? ____
Can you afford to lose the money if it fails? ____
Does the lease make it viable? ____
Do you have the ideal staff? ____
Is parking adequate? ____
How much do you know about the business? ____
Can you start small and expand? ____
Do you understand the marketing of the restaurant? ____
Have you always wanted to have a restaurant? ____
Does it fit in with your life goals? ____
Do you have the training? ____
Do you have adequate experience? ____
Are you a self-starter? ____

Do you like to work hard? ____
Do you enjoy the business? ____
Does your family like the idea? ____
Does your gut feeling say this is a good idea? ____

If you rank five of these variables with less than a 5, forget the project. Obviously if you have straight 10s, the project is a go.

ANOTHER CASE HISTORY

You have a job. It's not perfect, but it's a good job. You are considering another job. Should you take it?

This analysis would be a comparison: Current Job versus Future Job. Once again, before you can analyze the variables, you would have to do some sleuthing to discover the politics at the company you are considering. One subtle way to get information about a company is to locate the local bar the junior- and lower-middle managers frequent and go there. After a few drinks—their drinks, not yours—you can uncover substantial information.

Also talk to competitors and find out what the industry gossip is. If the company is public, get copies of the last three annual reports and current quarterly reports to analyze its financial strength and its potential weaknesses. Contact leading brokerage firms and request stock-analyst reports that scrutinize the company.

Then take a sheet of paper and rank these variables from 1 to 10 for your Current Job versus your Future Job.

	CURRENT	FUTURE
The industry is growing.	_____	_____
The company is growing.	_____	_____
You have the experience.	_____	_____
The company has a history of promoting women.	_____	_____

	CURRENT	FUTURE
It is the safest alternative.	_____	_____
Working there fits into your life strategy.	_____	_____
The job is one of your objectives.	_____	_____
The work load is one you like.	_____	_____
The boss is high on you.	_____	_____
The work environment suits you.	_____	_____
You enjoy the work.	_____	_____
The salary is great.	_____	_____
Prospects for raises are great.	_____	_____
It offers you the level of security you like.	_____	_____
Your future is bright.	_____	_____
It is a building block to your next job.	_____	_____
It is visible.	_____	_____
You are challenged in ways you enjoy.	_____	_____
The amount of required travel fits your life-style.	_____	_____
You like the boss.	_____	_____
The amount of entertaining fits your life-style.	_____	_____
The commute is easy.	_____	_____
The perks are better.	_____	_____
The hours required are to your liking.	_____	_____
The company is receptive to women beyond this level.	_____	_____
Very few people in this job have been fired at the company.	_____	_____
The problems are more interesting.	_____	_____
Your colleagues are more congenial.	_____	_____
Your gut tells you you should be there.	_____	_____

Compare the results of any variables that are most important to you. For instance, if you have a family, the hours would be an important consideration. If it's a lousy job that pays well and you want to amass some savings to be able to make a down payment on a new house, you might decide that the company is best for you despite the fact that many other variables are less than ideal. Or if you are miserable in your current job, you may decide that any alternative is welcome.

The judgment is ultimately yours. But if you add up your scores and one company ranks substantially ahead of the other, your decision is already made for you.

SCOLLARD'S LAW Quantifying variables brings alternatives into clear focus.

HOW TO DECIDE

Making decisions is not easy for most people. You can make the process far more effective if you take the time to do the homework that will give you the background to ask the right questions and calculate the odds.

Don't be reluctant to use your friends as a sounding board. They will each bring their own perspective to the judgment and you can learn from them.

Also seek out expert advice whenever you can. Advises Boston psychiatrist Ralph Hirschowitz, an expert in decision counseling, "If it looks simple, get someone to complicate it. If it looks complicated, get someone to simplify it. And be sure that reason is in the saddle and not emotion." A good decision is informed, evaluated, and cool. Don't use uncommon sense if plain old common sense will do.

Keeping a cool head is important. If you're emotional about a risk, back off until you cool down and are able to decide with intelligence instead of emotion.

Where you are in your life at a particular moment is an important consideration. When you're young and have nothing to lose, you will take risks that are different from when you have many responsibilities and substantial assets to lose. A young entrepreneur says that when she opened her business it was "all risk. No security. It didn't bother me at all because I was twenty-six, single, a Washingtonian who could make a phone call to get a job if things didn't work out."

"The more you have to lose, the more conservative you should be," suggests stock market analyst Richard Russell. He suggests that you consider what percentage of your assets you will have to risk to accomplish a goal.

Consider the possible outcome well in advance of taking a risk. If the salary demand you intend to make will cost you your job, be prepared to leave *before* you level your ultimatum. One entrepreneur says, "If my business didn't work, I could always do something. I could wait tables. I could convince somebody to give me a job doing something until I got myself together to do whatever it was that comes up next." She was emotionally prepared to deal with the worst possible case.

THE BEST CASE VERSUS THE WORST

Whenever you are making a decision about a risk, you should weigh the Best Possible Case versus the Worst Possible Case. Can you live with the Worst Possible Case? What are the odds of one or the other occurring? What is the Most Probable Case? After weighing the options, you should then evaluate the two possible extremes and whether the risk is worth taking.

With the restaurant we examined, the Best Possible Case would be that it is a smashing success. You make all your money back in the first year. And you prosper exceedingly. The Worst Possible Case would be that nobody comes—ever. You lose money from day one. And you go bankrupt. The odds are probably 1 in 10 that you would have the Worst Possible Case. And 1 in 10 that you would experience the Best Possible Case. So the odds are fairly even on the best and the worst. The Most Probable Case is that the restaurant would find its niche and slowly build so that you are making money in two or three years. The odds of that occurring are 1 in 3 to 1 in 6, depending on your experience and economic variables. This is easier to live with. But the question you always have to ask yourself is whether the probable reward is worth the risk.

When it comes to changing jobs, the Best Possible Case could be one of two alternatives, since we are considering two different companies. With your current employer, the Best Possible Case would be that you are promoted tomorrow, given a $10,000 raise, and told you are being groomed for the presidency. The Worst Possible Case would be that you would get fired. The odds of the former occurring, however, might be 1 out of 100 and the odds of the latter might be 1 in 10. The Most Probable Case would be that things continue pretty much as they are for the foreseeable future. The odds for that might be even.

At your future employer the Best Possible Case might be similar and the odds might be similar. The Worst Possible Case would be that you are fired on the first day. The odds for that might be 1 in 20. The Most Probable Case would be that you enter at a slightly higher level with the prospect of a larger salary. The odds for that might be 2 to 1. In that case, the future company gets the nod, assuming the other variables are similar.

SCOLLARD'S LAW The Worst Possible Case is the source of our worst fear. The Best Possible Case is our fondest hope.

RISK QUOTIENT

You can use your worst-case/best-case analysis to quantify the risks you are considering. There are six steps to follow to calculate the RQ of a risk.

- Describe the best-case outcome and worst-case outcome for a specific decision. Ideally, quantify it in dollars.

  EXAMPLE: You are employed by International Widget at an annual salary of $30,000. You have an opportunity at work to produce a prototype for a new widget. If you produce it on time and under budget, you get a $5,000 bonus. If you fail, you probably won't get even the 5 percent raise you would normally expect.

- Then assign a number to the probability of successfully achieving your goal. Remember to break the goal into as many distinct steps as appropriate.

  EXAMPLE: You believe that projects like this are completed on time 9 times out of 10—90 percent. You estimate that you have 7 chances in 10 of coming in under budget. You must *multiply* these probabilities to come up with a best-case chance of 63 percent.

- Multiply best-case outcome by best-case probability to arrive at best-case value.

  EXAMPLE: $5,000 × 63 percent = $3,150

- Calculate the worst-case probability by subtracting the best case from 100 percent.

  EXAMPLE: 100 percent − 63 percent = 37 percent

  Note: This represents the chance of *either* delivering the project late *or* over budget *or* both.

- Multiply the worst-case outcome by the worst-case probability to arrive at the worst-case value.

  EXAMPLE: Your 5 percent raise is worth $1,500; $1,500 × 37 percent = $555.

- Divide the best-case value by the worst-case value.

  EXAMPLE: 3150 \ 555 = Risk Quotient of 5.67

Any RQ greater than 1 is a good risk. Any RQ greater than 5 is a great one.

Consider the score you totaled up in chapter 2 when you consider an RQ. If you scored in the high 80s, you can handle any reasonable RQ. In fact you may have to consciously rein yourself in to avoid taking foolhardy risks. But if you scored in the 70s, you are probably not comfortable with an RQ greater than 3. If your scores are below 60, you should try to stick with RQs as close to 5 as possible. Since you are faint of heart, you want to try to keep your risks as close to a "sure thing" as you can while you build your confidence and ability.

WOMEN DECIDE

When you talk to successful risk takers, you occasionally find some who won against the odds. For instance, a woman who opened a vintage-clothing retail store recalls that she wasn't at all confident she would succeed. "We didn't know if the location would be right. I wasn't sure how people would react to the clothing. It all fell into place."

Generally women who are successful are much more cautious. Pam Fletcher-Hafemann, who has a beauty salon in Oceanside, California, says that she takes risks only if the worst possible case is not bad at all. She risked opening a second salon in a nearby town, figuring that she was unlikely to lose money. She didn't. But she did not make enough to make it worth the effort. "We could do it without losing money. And it gave us an opportunity to learn about how to expand," comments Fletcher-Hafemann.

Rosemary Garbett, a successful Houston restaurateur, says, "I try to eliminate as many factors that would cause it to fail before I do anything." Before she even puts a new entrée on the menu, she checks out her competition and says, "I eat a lot of it first." After opening a series of successful restaurants, she feels the risk is minimal. "For me to open a restaurant is not a gamble. I can physically get in and make it work myself." Of course she does her homework. "I have to negotiate the right lease. The numbers have to be right."

SCOLLARD'S LAW Most successful risk takers operate with the odds in their favor.

DUMB RISKS

After you've thought about it, it becomes easy to spot dumb risks. A stock market expert says, "Going to Las Vegas to bet or going to the races is pretty dumb. The odds are against you. If you play long enough, you're going to end up losing." He also thinks it would be dumb for a Jewish couple to open a mom-and-pop grocery store in a black neighborhood: The margins are thin at best, and the racial factor would be a further deterrent to business success.

An entrepreneur thinks it would be "dumb if you do a business everybody else is already doing." She has been successful innovating new ideas. She believes in being the first one in an area to develop a business concept.

Merry Clark, an executive in corporate America, thinks it would be dumb to react to pettiness. "To respond to pettiness and react foolishly is not thinking. Wait until your anger subsides. Don't be impulsive. Don't get mad. Get even. Have a plan and stick to it."

Another entrepreneur thinks it would be dumb to buy a business you know nothing about and are not interested in. "You have to love it to make it work," she says.

SCOLLARD'S LAW Your common sense is the best guide to spotting dumb risks.

SMART RISKS

Steven C. Leuthold, who has his own successful investment consulting firm, says it's smart to find a business that fits you. "Find a business that's as much fun as a hobby. You should love it. If you do, you're going to work a lot harder," he notes.

An executive says it's smart to watch the timing of the risks you take in a corporation. "Should I do it now or wait? Will it benefit me? Only take risks if they benefit you," she advises.

SCOLLARD'S LAW   Why take a dumb risk when it's so easy to spot smart ones?

CHARACTERISTICS OF DUMB RISKS

There is no research on which to judge.
The odds are staggeringly against you.
It was an emotional decision.
It makes you unhappy.
Your family hates it.
You are about to change your entire life at one time.
You aren't paying attention.
You've got to make a lot of effort for a small return.
You're doing it because you are angry.
The Worst Possible Case is 100 times worse than the Best Possible Case.

CHARACTERISTICS OF SMART RISKS

It is fun.
It makes you happy.
You've researched it for months.
The timing is right.
You are being as objective as you can possibly be.
You have given it your undivided attention.
Your family likes it.
It works to your advantage.
It's worth the risk.
It's worth the effort.
It makes sense.
The experts support you.
It fits the rest of your life.
Your gut likes it.

Build Your
Courage

IT IS ONLY NATURAL to suffer misgivings when you are taking risks. There's always the moment when you are out on a limb wondering, "It is the best thing for me to be here—isn't it???" Even the staunchest of successful risk takers has a few bad moments. Even with all the techniques in the world for dealing with stress, the anxiety is not going to go away. With an ache in the pit of your stomach and with many a sleepless night, you proceed anyway.

The ability to look your demons in the face and proceed even though you are terrified is one of the things that sets you apart as a risk taker.

The reality is that no matter how much homework you do, no matter how carefully you prepare yourself for a new venture, once you commit yourself to it and act on it, you are vulnerable. It isn't the things you can control that frighten you, it's the unexpected that creates the misery.

One of the main reasons you should be so careful in your planning for certain risks, so cautious and so prepared, is that Murphy's Law is the major force in the life of risk takers: What can go wrong usually does. And usually what goes wrong is always one of the things you took for granted. Whether it be the weather, acts of God, the fickle vagaries of the economy—who knows what can go wrong. It's the "who knows?" that can make you prematurely gray.

Indeed, most people only fantasize about taking risks successfully. They retreat to the packaged safe risks of video games and adventure movies. For a big thrill they seek out amusement and adventure on a roller coaster ride. "Wow, that was exciting," they say, and go home to their comfortable armchair.

The risk taker settles for no such cheap thrills. The roller coaster is not a carnival ride for her. It is everyday life. There's a lot at stake, and the excitement is nonstop.

Incidentally, some risk takers extend their risks beyond their businesses. Sometimes they seek thrills in their varied love lives or in the speed of a motorcycle or the challenge of an experimental aircraft. But not necessarily. Other risk takers prefer quiet lives outside of their businesses, peaceful, with gardens and cats.

FEAR

We all have our private demons. One woman's fear is another woman's joke. Our fears are as individual as we ourselves are. Just as there are no perfect bodies, there are no perfect psyches. Everyone is afraid of something. The important thing is not to let fear paralyze us into inactivity.

Sometimes you might think that by taking no risk you can avoid fear and live a safe, secure life. You frequently hear tales of people who let fear of risk taking propel them into a career in the slow lane. They keep "safe" low profiles in large corporations, never demanding much of a salary and never changing jobs. Times change, but they don't. The business is acquired or squeezed into retrenchment by a changing economy, and those people are casualties of the change. So much for the safety of taking few risks.

So we see, it is far riskier ultimately for people not to take what they perceive as risks. Their fear of the unknown makes them captives. The world changes, and they don't. Nothing is riskier than being out of pace in a changing marketplace.

"The people who succeed are the ones who put their fears on hold and move ahead, whether they have confidence or not," observes Patricia Harrison. "Everyone's afraid of something. But the people who don't let that fear block them are the ones who succeed." Continues Harrison, "But we look at them and think, well, these people are successful because they're smarter, are more attractive, or because they know the secret of success. But the real reason is that they're not waiting to become smarter or more attractive or to know any secrets. They're not waiting for, for instance, the right administration to come in or the weather to be perfect. They just do. They begin."

There are unknowns in any risk. You just have to gather your courage and at the most auspicious possible moment take action. Says a stockbroker, "It's similar to the time I fell overboard from a boat and thought, I wonder if there are sharks here." Then I realized that that was a most impractical thought, because if there were no sharks there, it was a waste to worry. And if there were sharks there, it was also a waste to worry."

Reasons Blanchet, "There are lines of thinking that people indulge in that really don't get them anywhere. They really can't afford them." When the urge to fret over some matter comes up, Blanchet suppresses it. "I'd say to myself, Gosh, I hope I don't need to worry about that."

It's important to recognize that worry can be useful if it is something you can control. But if you're overboard, it's not productive to worry about the sharks. Instead you should be worrying about swimming ashore—that you can control.

That's not to say you won't suffer. When Christine Foster decided to leave the convent and take up a secular life, she says, intense soul-searching preceded her move. "I agonized. I would cry myself to sleep at night before I made this decision, because it was a life choice, this was a divorce. I wasn't divorcing God, but I was divorcing a life-style. I agonized because I knew where I was going to be at age forty and I didn't want my life to be that pat. I needed more challenge in my life than the convent was going to provide."

Necessity is a good incentive. Says Harriett Berman, who opened a successful boutique in Los Angeles, "It was a last-ditch effort before I would have to go out and get a job. I'd been divorced five years. Alimony ran out in March, and it was really an act of, 'This is it. I have to support myself and my child and I have to make money.' So I was absolutely determined to make it work. I didn't want to get a job—I'm not skilled at anything."

Instead of being an employee, she puts her considerable people skills to work for her in her own store.

You fear the unknown, the things you think you cannot control. You can approach your fear constructively. Relates an entrepreneur, "My definition of fear is the lack of control. Anytime you feel like you're totally in control of what is going on, you have no fear. So, okay, be in control. And the more in control you are, the higher your self-esteem, the higher your confidence, and the more fearless you become."

Arna Vodenos, another successful entrepreneur, agrees. "It was mostly fear that taught me control. Because when you're afraid, you take your steps very carefully. In my first year I did everything myself. I thought about a low overhead. As I grew, I learned to trust others and delegate work. Now I have no fear. I'm always aware of the down side, but fear never holds me back."

Often your fear is based on your ego. "My big fear is that I won't be the best. I want to be the best. That's me," declares a corporate executive. "I experience uncertainty about the unknown, but what I don't fear is not being able to do the job. What I fear is not being successful—really successful—at it. At least I know I'm going to be above average, because most people don't have my drive."

Many people fear a loss of face, especially before a large audience. Jan Duval, who was the production manager for President Reagan's live appearances on television, says her own high standards created fear. "Part of me is very obsessive-compulsive. I really want it to be perfect."

One of the interesting things about women is that we take risks in some parts of our lives without any pause and then are terrified about other aspects. For instance, you may blithely run off and marry some man you hardly know—a major risk—and then stall at changing jobs because the risk seems too great.

Or you may take risks in your business and balk at commitments in your personal life. That is the case of Christine Dolan, former political director at Cable News Network (CNN). "I don't have professional fear. If I have fear of anything, it's the fear of having a broken heart. Of surrendering in a personal relationship."

Risks can be taken in your career in many different ways: going for a promotion, changing companies, making a dramatic career change, leaving a company to start your own, starting several new ventures.

Part of any fear is a lack of self-confidence, a dread of your inability to have adequate resources to meet the challenges, your inability to know exactly what those challenges might be.

Almost all of us harbor insecurities—it's a matter of degree. Jan Duval, who was trusted by President Reagan and his staff because of her excellence under duress, says, "I really feared my insecurity of not having a TV background. I feared that a Columbia master's degree (which has a superb production program) could walk in and do a better job."

Duval decided to change her career and become a psychotherapist, but she was once again lacking in confidence. She is a wonderful example of how foolish one's insecurities and lack of confidence look to someone else. Duval had managed the pressure of the press conferences of the most important man on the planet with professional ease and yet she panicked on her application for graduate school. "I was so nervous about applying because I really planned on it, I really wanted to get into Fordham. I looked at the application and noticed I had misspelled *psychology* three times. I was mortified. I called the school to say I spelled *psychology* wrong." She was accepted and, needless to say, was an outstanding student and is on her way to earning her master's.

The insecurities and lack of confidence you have may look ludicrous to someone else who views you as talented and exceedingly capable. Edith Fierst, for example, studied law but opted to be a full-time housewife and mother for a few years. During that time her professional confidence crumbled. She admits, "I had zero confidence when I started my career. I thought I didn't know anything. I got a volunteer job at the Legal Aid Society. Clients would come in and ask, 'What should I do?' Well, I didn't know what they should do. I was guessing. So when I finally began to look for a job, I had no confidence at all. My first job was in the Labor Department. I said, 'I represent a social problem and I think you should take me on. I have great credentials and can't find a part-time job.' I went to work at the same level as a secretary was doing. Five years later I got a job that I liked and felt good about being a lawyer."

SCOLLARD'S LAW   Our worst fears far outstrip our worst failures.

SUPPORT SYSTEM

To help yourself through difficult times you should consciously surround yourself with people who believe in you and support you in your risk taking. Spend as much of your time as possible with your supporters and take your detractors with a grain of salt.

Someone who has seen you in one role may be unable to see you as something else which you would become with your risk taking. Your mother-in-law may not be able to envision you as the head of your own business. Your brother may think you should never change jobs.

Sometimes it is necessary to change jobs to avoid being pigeonholed. For instance, if you start off as a company secretary and are promoted to a manager, some people in that business will always view you as a secretary, regardless of how well you perform. You should change jobs and move to another company. There you are perceived as a manager from the outset and not somebody who started out as Jean Smith's secretary.

Frequently people who have not overtly tackled the challenge of risk taking are the strongest detractors of those who do. "It'll never work." "You can't do that." "What makes you think you can do this?" are favorite phrases of the armchair observers, who are scared to death to do anything themselves.

When you are facing special risks, it is good to associate with people who have taken similar gambles and won. They are sure to cheer you on. Comments a woman who began her career at age forty, "Figure out what you want to do and then go after it like a pit bull. Go after it and don't let anybody tell you, 'Don't be silly. You can't do that.' Don't *ever* tell anybody that they won't be able to do it, it's not possible. Everything is possible, and dreams and goals are very important. Surround yourself with people like you want to be, people with a sense of self-worth."

Stay on the alert for role models. You don't even have to know them personally to learn from them. You see them being interviewed on television, written up in magazines and newspapers, giving speeches. Join civic and business associations and study the most successful people there. Listen to them carefully. Observe how they think, what their attitude is.

You may find that you need to find some new friends when you change your life by risk taking. One woman who decided to become self-employed found that her attitude and life-style changed with the transition. Her old friends were all miserable in their jobs and spent much of their time complaining. She found she preferred the company of other self-employed women, who tend to be much more upbeat and excited about their businesses.

It is hard for someone who has never dared to take business risks to appreciate what you're going through. Frequently you encounter, "I told you so," instead of sympathy. And there's nothing wrong with getting a little sympathy when you suffer setbacks. Seek out people who understand exactly what you're going through.

It is easier to succeed if your spouse or boyfriend is supportive. One now successful entrepreneur says that her boyfriend was "one hundred percent a motivating factor" in taking a risk to change her career. "He was a catalyst for getting me to the point of saying, 'Hey, play in the big leagues,'" she says.

Your parents can be a critical factor in how you view risks. Kaye Lani Rae Rafko, who was Miss America in 1988, says her family were her biggest fans. "They were very supportive and encouraging. They psych me up when I'm on stage. You can't help but hear them screaming in the crowd, 'Shake them up, Lani,' when I do the Tahitian dance," she says, referring to the talent number she performed in the competitions.

How you were raised as a child affects how you feel about risk taking. Recently-turned-entrepreneur Christine Dolan says, "My father is an entrepreneur. He is very pro women." Her father was "thrilled" when she left her job as political director at CNN and went out on her own. Another successful businesswoman points out that she also had a supportive family. "I was raised by liberal parents who told me I could do whatever I want to. It was never brought to my attention by them that anything was impossible." She feels the benefits of this attitude have been a tremendous asset. "I wish everyone could be blessed with parents like mine. I see a lot of people who go all the way to adulthood and still have a nagging feeling that somebody somewhere thought they were going to be a failure, so therefore they were."

You can turn childhood adversity into character building blocks. One woman credits some of her success to the hardships she had in childhood. "I was tall, and my mother died," she recalls. She found support in her sister and high school teachers.

SCOLLARD'S LAW   There's no such thing as too much support.

INNER STRENGTH

No matter how much support you get from other people, there is no substitute for your own inner strength. Ultimately the decision to take a risk is up to you. It's your life, and no one, no matter how supportive, can do it for you.

You may find that you don't even need a lot of cheering on the sidelines. Notes a successful attorney, "My husband wasn't interested in my work. As long as the house was run well, he didn't show interest in what I was doing. I had no choice but to work because of my personality. I just had to stick with it."

Nancy Blanchet didn't tell her family and friends about her work when she became a stockbroker. "I didn't tell anybody at first," she relates. "I didn't want to put my friends and neighbors in the embarrassing position of thinking I might ask them for their business," she says.

You may simply have to ignore what people tell you about your ability to succeed. Arna Vodenos says that people have tried to tell her that she couldn't have a career and a family life at the same time. "I'm trying to say I can do both," she declares. Another woman reports, "I found a lot of my girlfriends were a little jealous and weren't supportive."

Rebecca Tilton has been successful in the advertising agency she founded with a partner. "A black older gentleman and a young white female—there was no room in this market for that," recalls the now twenty-nine-year-old Tilton. Moreover, they began their business in 1984 when Denver was in a business recession. "We didn't have any money. We didn't have any clients. Sherman and I had a lot of contacts. Even my own friends— people I thought were my friends—snubbed me for going into business with a black man. And snubbed me when we got our first contract with the government." Tilton and her partner have been successful despite the lack of support. Last year their firm, Hamilton Tilton Advertising, had gross billings of $10 million. Tilton thrived on the challenges. "That's what makes me go," she declares.

SCOLLARD'S LAW   Inner strength is like a muscle: the more you flex it, the larger it becomes.

COURAGE–ENHANCING RITUALS

There are a variety of touchstones you can use to get you through the most difficult moments of risk taking. One woman writes down all the variables of a situation on a piece of paper. On one side she lists "Things I can control." On the other side she lists "Things that are out of my control." Then she tears the sheet down the middle and literally sets fire to the side with the things she cannot control. "There's no reason to worry about things I have no influence over," she says.

Your courage can be bolstered by using some of the following techniques:

- *Study yourself.* Be candid about your strengths and weaknesses. Position yourself so that your risks play off of your strengths. Be honest with yourself about your weaknesses, and if you have a partner or an ally in a venture, ideally you should have complementary strengths. One woman says, "My worst fault in risk taking is that I'm always pessimistic. But I know that. I know things are not going to go as badly as I fear. But my husband is the opposite. He is extremely optimistic. So we balance each other out."

  It is easier to succeed in your risk taking when you have reached your thirties. The reason is that it is easier to meet challenges after you are thoroughly acquainted with your personal assets and liabilities. After you have a strong sense of who you are, it is easier to take risks successfully. You should use your teens and twenties to explore yourself, to learn who you are and what you want out of life.

- *Imaging.* It is important that you permit yourself to dream, that you imagine yourself as having successfully hurdled multiple risks and obstacles to achieve your dream. This may be a private vision or one you share with only your closest friends or lover.

  You may have an image of yourself and recognize it only after you achieve a certain goal. For instance, I had no conscious dreams of achieving great corporate success when I was growing up. But when I first occupied my beautiful, spacious executive office as the first woman vice president in the history of then one-hundred-year-old Chesebrough-Pond's, the office seemed familiar and it seemed only natural that I should be sitting there. Then I remembered an old black-and-white movie I had seen on television in my youth in Nashville, Tennessee. It had been a movie where someone such as Barbara Stanwyck played a beautiful executive in a similar office. I realized I had had the image in the back of my mind for probably twenty years. It had been a powerful motivator.

  You can propel yourself to success by imagining yourself to be already there. Imagine how people will respond to you, how much you will enjoy the attention of having accomplished what you set out to do, how proud you will feel about having jumped the hurdles. In your darkest moments visit the image in your mind and caress it.

SCOLLARD'S LAW A dream usually inspires its own reality.

- *Past glories.* Success you've had in the past can strengthen your courage as you face new risks. You should sit down and list on a piece of paper at least three successes. They can be any kinds of success, from the birthday party you gave for your three-year-old last year to the way you negotiated the mortgage on your house. What is important is that you remember the successes you have had and remind yourself that there will be many more.

    When your courage is wavering and you are doubting yourself while you undergo new risks, make it easy to recall some of the many past hurdles you have cleared.

SCOLLARD'S LAW Give yourself plenty of credit. Stop to pat yourself on the back.

- *Assume consent.* After you commit yourself to a goal, assume that you will achieve it. Think positively. Project confidence. Keep your fears and anxieties to yourself.

    This is especially important if you have a team working with you. As a leader you should generate enthusiasm and optimism. You want to motivate your people to give a project their best and then hope for the best.

    Confidence is something you inspire in people by the way you conduct business and how you present yourself. It is something you should very consciously strive to elicit. It involves how you speak, dress, move, how your secretary behaves, and how your phone is answered.

SCOLLARD'S LAW The more people believe in you, the easier it becomes to believe in yourself.

HOW TO PROJECT
CONFIDENCE

Take a few deep breaths in private before a major meeting.

Look people directly in the eye.

Shake hands firmly.

Be positive. Don't say, "I think it is." Say, "It is."

Don't apologize if you are wrong. Admit it and rectify it immediately.

Be at least two minutes early for any important meeting.

Don't hesitate to answer your own phone.

Have your presentation typed up neatly. Hand out copies before you begin.

Take a course in public speaking.

Rehearse any important presentation until you've memorized it.

Don't fumble in your briefcase. Know where everything is and whip it out on cue.

Carry an expensive-looking writing pen.

Wear brilliant colors and/or black and white.

Wear bold costume jewelry or the real McCoy. (All rings should be the real McCoy).

If you don't know the answer, admit it. Find out as quickly as possible.

Cue your staff to be accessible by phone if you might need any backup information.

Hire a secretary with wonderful telephone rapport.

If you don't have a secretary, periodically buy candy and flowers for whoever answers your phone in your absence. You want them to always remember who you are.

If you use your car in business, treat it as an accessory. It should be immaculate.

Return all phone calls the same day. If possible, return all calls within four hours—regardless of where you are.

If you are traveling and no phone is accessible, instruct your secretary to return your call to see if she can be of any assistance in your absence.

When you are ill, return your calls from home. People are reassured when they know they can reach you.

Pay attention to all details.

Keep your personal problems to yourself. You don't want your boss or your client wondering if you are capable of handling a special project.

Keep abreast of current events.

Book your vacations well in advance. Time them to coincide harmoniously with the demands of your work.

Keep in touch with clippings and personal handwritten notes.

Always know what time it is.

Do your homework before any meeting. Surprise is not confidence building.

Under no circumstances resort to tears.

Keep a stash of spare stockings, needle and thread, and safety pins for emergencies.

- *Bluffing.* This is what you do much of the time early on while you hope you are inspiring confidence. One of the most surprising aspects of entrepreneurism and corporate life is the extent to which bluffing is an important ploy. You mask your fears. You act "cool, calm, and collected" under the most difficult of situations. In short, you fake it.

  By the same token, you take personal credit for serendipitous events, as though you had planned them. Windfalls are taken in stride as though planned. You never allude to your failures. It is as though they had never happened.

  Bluffing is an important aspect of the game of business and one that men generally play better. You are far more likely to hear a woman admit her fears than a man. In this instance, we should learn from men and emulate them. For example, if you are soliciting a contract for a project that is really more than you can imagine, you should never let on that you don't expect to get it. You walk in and make your pitch as though you are convinced you will get it. And then when you get it, you show no surprise, but merely comment how wise they were to award you the project. You shake hands, walk briskly out to your car, get in, roll up the windows. And then and only then you permit yourself to scream with delight.

By the same token, you ask for a raise with a straight face, even though you have no hope of getting one. When you actually do get it, you conceal your surprise. You save your expressions of glee for only your closest friends.

SCOLLARD'S LAW Playing a mean hand of gin rummy helps you win in business.

• *Luck.* Some people are born lucky. If you are, you know you are. If you're not, you know that, too. If you're not, team up with someone who is. If you work for someone, make sure you work for lucky bosses. Then it's easy. As they make all the right moves, you follow them right up the corporate ladder. They clear the way, and you ride in their wake.

If you want to have your own business and you don't feel lucky, find a lucky partner. Normally I advise against taking a partner, but in this instance you may be better off. If you feel decidedly unlucky and know someone who lives a charmed life, draw up a good partnership contract and hitch your wagon to a star.

I've always thought that you could make your own luck. One way is hard work. The saying is true: "The harder I work, the luckier I get." Hard work is far more satisfying than easy work. And work is far more desirable than idleness.

Luck has also been defined as being the instant where preparation meets opportunity. The preparation is what you are doing when you study a book such as you are now. Opportunity comes from keeping your eyes open. Keep in mind that opportunities usually have a right moment. Once that moment is gone, the opportunity is gone. For instance, because of the oil glut a couple of years ago there were many idle boats on the Gulf of Mexico that had previously serviced the oil rigs. When the oil rigs shut down, the boats to service them were no longer needed. The owners of the boats went bankrupt, and the boats went into dry dock. The banks ended up owning the boats, and they almost couldn't give them away. At that point you could buy a boat for 10 cents on the dollar. That means a $5-million boat could be purchased for $500,000. And businesses that would never have been viable if you had to spend $5 million for the boat in the first place became suddenly very profitable. Ferries, charters, transportation of building supplies—there was an opportunity to start a variety of shipping-related businesses. A lot of people did. Some people would say they were lucky. In fact, they were prepared to act and grabbed the opportunity.

That particular opportunity is gone—the market for boats has turned around—but there are new opportunities every day. You need to train yourself to see them. And you must prepare yourself in advance and then patiently wait for the right opportunity to present itself. Then you, too, can be lucky.

SCOLLARD'S LAW The only success stories that don't involve hard work are fairy tales.

METAMORPHOSIS

You can become anything you want to be. It is up to you. It is possible for a timid, insecure woman to become a gutsy risk taker. It takes awhile. But successful risk taking breeds increased risk taking. And success breeds confidence. And confidence breeds more success.

Says Becky Tedesco, who heads up her own temporary service, "Believe me, there's a difference in me right now from what was there five years ago. A big difference between what there is today and twenty years ago. In other words, no one can tell me anymore that there's something I can't do." She continues, "You get to a point where you realize that you aren't afraid of anyone or anything anymore. Then your confidence gets so high that you do things that ten years ago you wouldn't have dreamed you could do. It's a pyramid and it continues to grow."

Tedesco became president of Ameritemps by choice. She was motivated to succeed. To own her own business, she sold her house and borrowed money from her father. "I think some of us are spurred on to things because we are scared to death to fail at it. And that creates such a rush that you succeed. But I think if it comes too easily and you don't have your own personal worth invested in it, you may not be as successful as those who lay everything on the line."

Women become successful because they want to test their limits, to see how good they are, how far they can go.

Sometimes they are forced by circumstances. One woman became a hugely successful stockbroker because she had five children to feed and it seemed a likely way to earn a living. One woman with no work experience suddenly found herself a widow with four young children to support. Having decided to go into real estate, she flunked the exam the first couple of times. Frequently while the kids were in school, she sat at the kitchen table and cried in despair. But once she was licensed, she was a fireball. The first year she sold a million dollars worth of real estate. Now she owns a sizable real estate firm, has about fifty employees, and has sent all of her children through private schools.

Often you have no idea how much you can do until you've pushed yourself—or life has pushed you—to do it.

Persistence and determination are important characteristics. These qualities get you through the bleak, lonely moments when your misgivings are on the ascendant. You must not let yourself quit. Once you pass one hurdle, the next one is easier. Eventually, experienced at risk taking, you achieve goals that were beyond your wildest dreams. Says a successful Hollywood producer, "I have made major jumps, started companies, left secure surroundings a handful of times. I do it because the excitement of risk taking is a lot of fun and fairly addictive."

SCOLLARD'S LAW   Risk is the cocoon. Success is the butterfly.

Keeping Cool
Under Stress

YOU CAN BE SUCCESSFUL only to the
extent that you learn to manage stress. Look at the leaders in any
field, the most successful people. The one thing they all have in
common is that they've learned to deal with a considerable
amount of stress.

First of all it's important to recognize when you are feeling
stressed out. If you don't even know you are out of control, you
are not likely to focus on gaining control.

Study the following symptoms of stress and see which of them
you manifest.

Irritability: You tend to snap at people for no reason.

Hyperactivity: You pace, drum your fingers, grind your teeth.

Perspiration: You sweat more than usual.

Shakiness: Your hands tremble, your knees feel weak.

Dry mouth: You have difficulty swallowing—or you swallow
excessively.

Voice changes: The pitch moves up or down. You can hear
your stress in your voice. You wonder if other people notice.

Smoking: Normally a moderate smoker, you become a chain-
smoker. You start one cigarette before you finish your previous one. If you've stopped smoking, you take it up again.

Eating: You either lose your appetite or you eat compulsively.
Your eating habits dramatically change.

Caffeine: You drink tons of coffee or soft drinks. You feel you
need the extra boost.

Alcohol: You have more to drink in the evening. You feel it's the only way you can relax.

Cough: Under pressure you have a dry cough you can't control.

Anger: You fly off the handle for the darndest reasons. Your anger is misplaced, directed at some innocent source.

Impatience: You are angered by being put on hold or having to wait in line for gasoline for your car.

Rudeness: Amenities seem too cumbersome. You don't care if people don't understand, you have no time for being polite.

Abruptness: You change the subject for no reason, going time and again to the one that is bothering you.

Insomnia: Your problems keep you awake. You lie awake night after night.

Poor complexion: Your skin looks pasty. You break out in a rash.

Poor concentration: You have a difficult time focusing on the work you should be doing.

Nightmares: Even when you do sleep, you have terrible dreams that are as stressful as your waking life.

Loss of perspective: Small things take on extraordinary importance. You dwell on nonproductive matters. You can't think about anything else.

Lethargy: You feel fatigued. Accomplishing small tasks becomes a huge burden. All you want to do is sleep.

Depression: You actually feel suicidal. You feel hopeless and despairing.

Procrastination: You postpone tasks. You don't want to do anything. Everyday chores require a superhuman effort.

Whining: You hear yourself ranting and going on endlessly. You're always talking about the same thing.

Crying: For no reason you burst out into sobs. You see a sad movie and cry uncontrollably.

Forgetfulness: You can't remember something someone told you yesterday. You forget if you have already returned a phone call. You entirely forget a lunch engagement you made.

If you are exhibiting some of these symptoms, people are going to notice. And that attention will only create more stress for you. What you must do is learn to manage your stress. It is necessary before you can be in control of your life. When you are stressed out, you are not in charge. The situation rules you.

It's important to realize that your stress tolerance is as individual as your personality. Different people thrive on different levels of stress. And different things stress out different people.

"I'm the kind of person who works well with a lot of pressure. Without it I buckle under," says Asa Miller, who heads up Miller Marketing Network in New York City. "I'd rather have stress than boredom," comments a prominent Washington, D.C.–based attorney. She says she tends to take on too much. "There're always things I like to do, so I find myself getting overinvolved and I feel stress. But I'm old enough and experienced enough that I can balance much of what I do."

Some people do every day what other people have nightmares about. "I have stress when I'm hanging out of a plane to get a good shot," matter-of-factly declares photographer Carol Highsmith.

It's important to recognize that you are the cornerstone of your own existence and that how you feel determines much of your success in risk taking. One hardworking woman notes, "I feel stable, therefore if everything else is falling apart, I'm still okay." She acknowledges that she knows certain situations that would be very stressful for her. "I think if I had to worry about how I was going to pay the bills, that would do me in more than anything. I live on less than what I'm making, so I don't have the stress of money problems." What she is doing is very healthy. She has identified one worry that would really upset her and she avoids it. Therefore she does not have to adjust to what would be for her an unpleasant degree of stress.

You should do the same for yourself. You should sit down and analyze what kinds of things are most stressful for you and eliminate them from your life.

TV executive Lynn Loring says she has learned to deal with the stress of an uncertain future. "I find myself much less concerned about things like: What if I'm not earning this much money next year? What if I can't afford to do this? What if I lose my job? My mother, the older generation, says, 'Can you afford that house? What if you're not earning that kind of money three years from now?' Well, if I'm not earning that kind of money three years from now, I'll sell the house. Life will go on. Life is not easy. It's not a picnic."

Loring's job is a high-stress one, and she thrives on it. "I live with stress. It's a part of life. Someone once asked me what would I do without stress. I would probably create it."

Continues Loring, "One of the problems is knowing what true stress is, what true problems are, and not turning the little problems into major ones—which I have a great tendency to do. Sometimes the cleaner loses a dress for a day, and I can get more psycho about that than a show getting bad ratings. I find it hard not to make my kids or friends responsible for an insane director or writer. It's very easy to misplace anger, to misplace stress."

Recognizing the problem, of course, is the key to solving it. Make a list of the things that stress you out the most. Here, for instance, is my list:

1. Uncertainty about my future schedule
2. Being yelled at for no reason
3. Being yelled at for good reason
4. Impossible deadlines
5. Unreliable employees
6. Disagreements with my boyfriend
7. Car accidents and breakdowns
8. Coming home to an empty house
9. Having a negative cash flow

Now that I've made the list, the issue becomes, What can I do to alleviate the possibility of having to deal with these things that would be stressful? Simple. I design my life so that I have some control over these things and so that the possibility of these stresses occurring is lessened.

1. My schedule: I have a first-rate assistant, who is superb at nailing down my schedule. My plans are completely in her capable hands.

2. Being yelled at: I walk away.

3. Being yelled at for good reason: I walk away and give myself a pep talk.

4. Impossible deadlines: I don't make them for myself. And I don't accept them. But I do procrastinate sometimes and put myself in a tough deadline situation.

5. Unreliable employees: This is harder to control. I hire the best I can. When they let me down, I feel stressed. But it doesn't happen very often.

6. Disagreements with my boyfriend: I found one who hates to argue as much as I do.

7. Car accidents and breakdowns: I maintain my vehicles as conservatively and preventively as possible. I know people who are reliable I can call on if I am in an accident or should a breakdown occur.

8. Empty house: I have cats, who are delighted to see me whenever I return.

9. Money: I budget conservatively. I try to give myself a 20 percent margin. If I don't need it, I invest it.

This exercise shows you how simply I've dealt with some of the problems that I really dislike dealing with. This leaves me free to focus my energies on doing business and solving the inevitable problems that arise there. But I've eliminated many unnecessary stresses so that I don't feel stressed out.

You probably also noticed that some of the things that I have discovered stress me out don't bother you in the slightest. That's important to recognize. Don't apologize for your stress points. Just fix them. Take control of your life.

Says an advertising executive, "Without a balance and being in touch with your personal values and your own personal commitment you're not going to do your job, your business, or whatever any good. We always tend to look at them separately. We have to look at them as a whole part of you."

It's important to recognize that stresses have cumulative effects. Thus if you argue with your husband or child in the morning, have a small accident on the way to work, get yelled at by your boss who is in a lousy mood, and get a call from the bank notifying you that you are overdrawn, you are bringing a lot of stress to the office with you. Then, if clients move up your deadline for getting a proposal to them, you are going to feel a great deal of stress.

What can you do? First of all you should recognize what is happening to you. Then eliminate as much of the stress as you quickly can. Call your husband and make up. Forget the car for the time being; it runs and you can fix it when there's nothing else bad happening in your work. Give yourself a pep talk, pointing out that your boss is stressed out and taking it out on you. Call your bank and transfer some money from your savings account and get to work on the important stress: giving your client what he or she wants.

What you are doing is freeing yourself to focus on the major problem at hand. You have reduced the amount of pressure you feel and very likely will do a better job.

There's no reason to try to be superwoman and take on all the stress of the world at one time. No one appreciates the burden that you are bearing, and it hinders you in your effectiveness.

Admit that you are only human. Ask for help if you feel overwhelmed. This may be difficult for you, because many successful risk takers convince themselves that they can handle absolutely anything. And their pride gets in the way. One successful risk taker readily admits she is very tough on herself. "Unfortunately I'm not a person that's very able to ask for help. That's one of my personal character traits. I'm stubborn and I don't have the ability to ask for help even when I really need it."

When you feel stressed out, make a list of all the things creating pressure for you. Eliminate as many as possible. And resolve as many issues as you possibly can. Notes a free-lance writer, "The more you can clear out, whether it's a problem with a relative or a bad experience, it frees you up and gives you so much energy. You'd be surprised how much energy it takes to keep it inside."

Becky Tedesco, president of her own firm, Ameritemps, agrees. "I'm an instant stress releaser," she says. "When a problem comes to me, I jump on it immediately. I'm not a person to sit back and mull over it. When there's a problem, I attack it immediately.

And I get it all out. It doesn't matter if it's a personal problem or a business problem, when a problem arises, jump on it immediately."

Tedesco's point is well taken. By dealing with problems immediately you free yourself up to deal with any new pressures that come along. It is easier for you to stay focused.

One of the negative aspects of stress is that it can actually make you sick. You see it all the time. A woman breaks up with her boyfriend and she immediately gets the flu or a cold.

Being aware of the relationship between stress and illness can help you protect yourself. If you are changing jobs or getting a divorce, be especially kind to yourself. Be alert for any early symptoms and get plenty of rest. The challenge is to get through a stressful period without making yourself sick.

Positive events can be as stressful as negative ones. Getting married, getting a promotion, going on vacation—all these things create stress too. A survey by one physician indicated that 90 percent of the cancer patients he interviewed had undergone changes in their lives within the previous twenty-four months. These changes were both negative, such as a death in the family, and positive, such as receiving a promotion.

It is important that you be aware of the correlation between stress and illness and protect yourself as much as possible.

If you don't, you can end up in the same boat twenty-eight-year-old advertising whiz Rebecca Tilton found herself in: "I did not know how to relax. I did not know how to take time for myself. I could not relax even when I tried. I was so stressed. So high-strung. I just pushed my health back."

There are six different techniques to help you manage stress. You should practice them and make them part of your everyday life, practicing them until they become second nature.

HUMOR

"Laugh before you cry," advises one executive. When things are getting tense, humor can defuse a charged situation. A good laugh restores perspective. An entrepreneur says she relies on humor to alleviate stress. "I don't take things as seriously anymore. I can laugh at myself a lot more easily now. I went through periods of my life where I couldn't really laugh because I took it too seriously. There are good days and bad days and you go through them. Dropping dead because of a bad day is crazy. So I handle stress with a self-deprecating sense of humor because I know the stress that's there is only how I view life. It's going to be stressful if I say it's going to be stressful. I'm not saying to ignore stress. A lot of change can be stressful. You have to be realistic about certain changes, but maintain your sense of humor."

Humor is healthy because it restores a sense of perspective. Often you feel stressed because it seems the issue at hand is all-important and critical. By laughing you bring a different view to the situation. It may be black humor, but it is better than none at all.

Treat your work stresses as a game. Don't respond to every deadline or every crisis as though it were a life-and-death matter. Every person's tolerance for stress is different. Design a work style that has stresses that you tolerate well. If you have a job or a business that makes you miserable, change it. There is no reason to continue in a life-style that makes you unhappy.

Observe the stresses the people around you are in and identify the stress-induced patterns they exhibit. Use this information to keep your perspective when you are on the receiving end of some of that behavior, such as irritability, rudeness, and hyperactivity.

Humor is an invaluable aid to defusing the situation with someone who is stressed out. The right amount of levity, dropped in just at the right minute, can completely turn around what was previously a negative situation.

Be sure you use a light hand with your humor. Often, when people are stressed out, they completely lose their sense of humor. Make sure you don't alienate an angry client by appearing not to take his rage seriously.

It is a reasonable objective to resolve to always keep your sense of humor. At least you can laugh in the bleakest of times.

SCOLLARD'S LAW   When you don't know whether to laugh or cry, be sure that you opt for laughter.

DELEGATING

Women don't have it all. We *do* it all. Don't. At home you should use the delegating skills that serve you so well at the office. Don't try to do everything yourself.

The reason we have so much to do is that we still carry the lion's share of responsibilities for our families and our husbands. Our greatest liability is that we'll never have a wife. We *are* the wives. We often fall into the trap of trying to be all things to all people. And the result is that we have absolutely no time for ourselves and feel extremely stressed out.

It is important that we set our priorities and decide which things are the most important and that we let some things go. You quickly decide to let certain things slide. For instance, one woman says, "The first thing I let go was having a clean house. The next thing was a home-cooked dinner. I get take-out dinners a few days and then cook lots of vegetables on the weekend to make up for all the junk food I let the kids eat during the week." Another woman observes, "I haven't washed my windows in three years. That priority just never quite makes it to the list."

Be sure that you include yourself in your priorities. In the scramble to be wife, mother, and career person you may find that it's very difficult to allocate time for yourself. Schedule time for yourself in your day as though it were for an important client. One woman schedules her workout at five-thirty and treats it as seriously on her calendar as she would cocktails with a major client. When something comes up to interfere with that time for herself, she schedules around it. It is only rarely that she relinquishes that time for herself.

SUGGESTED GOODS AND
SERVICES TO DELEGATE

Sending out clothes to the laundry
Fast food
Take-out food
Bakeries
Courier services
Packing and shipping services
People to wait in line for you
Housecleaning services
Someone to wait for the repairman for you
Laundries that repair clothes and sew on snaps and buttons
Manicurist to come to office or home
Massage person to come to office
Gardener
Caterer
Someone to organize your closets
Personal shopper
Laundry pickup and delivery
Garage that picks you up, services car, and delivers it to your
    office
First question: "Do you deliver?"
Vet who makes house calls
Dog walker
Answering machine
Grocery store delivery

The first things you delegate are the things you hate to do. If
you hate housekeeping, the first person you hire is a housekeeper.
If you hate waiting for the car to be serviced, find a garage that
handles it for you. Ironing, cooking, cleaning are chores that are
frequently delegated.

Be creative in your delegation. Ask people, "Will you do that for me?" "Will you deliver?" "Will you do that for me at home at 9 P.M.?" Avail yourself of every service you can afford.

Find out what the expectations of your family are. One woman determinedly baked a cake for her son's birthday because she thought it was important for him. One year she simply could not, so she bought one at a local bakery. Much to her chagrin, she discovered he thought the purchased cake was far superior to the ones she had baked over the years. She then realized she had wasted a great deal of time.

Another woman tested the limits of what she could delegate with her husband. She discovered that he didn't mind if the housekeeper cooked their dinners. All he expected of his wife was that she warm it up in the microwave and serve it to him. (He is under the erroneous impression that his wife seasons the food. She leaves him with his illusions.)

Frequently you find that you're knocking yourself out to do something for your family when they really don't care. Often you think something is important when it isn't. Find out what is important and limit yourself to those tasks.

When you're delegating, be sure that you keep for yourself the tasks that make you feel good about yourself. Analyze yourself and see which tasks make you feel feminine or happy. For instance, if baking Johnny's cake makes you feel good about yourself, then bake it, whether Johnny cares or not. If preparing elaborate meals relaxes you and makes you feel good, then by all means prepare meals. You may find that you cook on weekends and holidays when you have time and settle for prepared food the rest of the week. The same is true of gardening. If you enjoy puttering with your flowers, don't delegate it, save it for yourself and delegate something else.

The ideal you should seek is one where you mostly do things that you enjoy and delegate the others. This reduces your stress considerably because you are designing your life so that you are spending most of your time doing things you really enjoy. You are in control.

It is important to keep a clear view of your priorities. The point is to have a good life. Factor your femininity into the equation. For instance, perhaps you shower in the mornings because it takes less time. If you enjoy baths, schedule one on the weekend. Indulge yourself. Don't let small things interfere with that indulgence.

It is a good idea to set up a reward system for yourself to compensate you for doing things you don't like. The system should be direct. The reward should be on a 1-to-1 ratio. For instance, if you've spent three hours with a difficult, abusive client, reward yourself with three hours doing something that you really enjoy doing and rarely take the time to do, whether it's getting a facial or visiting a friend. If you enter a stressful situation knowing that you will give yourself a happy reward afterward, the stress is more easily put into perspective.

Or you can reward yourself by buying yourself presents. For instance, a woman who has a very unpleasant client purchased herself an expensive bracelet, which she named her "Denise bracelet," named after the difficult client. Whenever the woman sees that client, she is certain to wear the bracelet. It cheers her immeasurably every time she looks at it. Of course, the client is oblivious of the situation. The client is no less problematic, but the stress has been handled. The bracelet helps the woman keep the grief her client gives her in perspective.

SCOLLARD'S LAW   Design your life so that you spend much of your time doing things you enjoy doing.

SCOLLARD'S LAW   Be very good to yourself.

DIVERSION

Stresses and problems are easier to deal with if you gain perspective. One easy way to gain a fresh viewpoint is to turn away from the problem and let your subconscious work on it while you do something else. "I get up and walk away from stressful situations," notes a successful Chicago businesswoman. "I read, listen, talk, and concentrate on something else for a while. Then I go back to my stress with fresh eyes." One woman says she telephones her children to regain perspective. Another works a crossword puzzle.

Frequently a good night's sleep helps you gain a clearer viewpoint on a problem. Let your subconscious work for you. Tackle the fundamentals of a problem and then put it out of your conscious mind for a while. Chances are it will be much easier to solve after your subconscious has wrestled with it. One woman studies the details of a problem and then goes jogging, listening to New Age music. She says she's usually solved the problem by the time that she has run her daily three or four miles.

Says realtor Nancy Helmer, "To help keep stress under control, I put things in perspective. If something is eating at me, I ask the question: No matter which way this turns out, is it going to matter in five or ten years from now? If it doesn't, you've got to let go of it and do whatever you can to work it out. If it matters five or ten years from now, then that's where you'll have to make your efforts and be concerned." This philosophy keeps her focused on the most important matters. She notes, "Some people get involved in inconsequential things, and when something really important comes along, they can't handle it."

SCOLLARD'S LAW With a fresh perspective, problems appear substantially smaller.

ESCAPES

There's much to be said for a proverbial change of scenery. Vacations and weekends are one of the saving graces of many a successful life. "I go to the country and put business completely out of my mind," says one corporate president, who takes her husband and young daughter along with her.

Going home and being a mother and wife is refreshing because it presents you with a totally different set of stresses. Stockbroker Nancy Blanchet describes her life as a stockbroker and parent as "always extremely schizophrenic." "As I would drive home, I always figured that by the time I hit the zoo, I couldn't be a broker anymore. I was Mother. So, when I arrived home, I was into that role. I just didn't think about the job at all by the time I was halfway home."

Blanchet simply steps from one role into the other. "If you have a job that is too big, you have to try to control it. Otherwise it will be overwhelming."

An executive in a high-stress job says that her home is her sanctuary. "My home is my womb. The minute I walk through that door, I leave my work problems behind me. I screen my phone calls at home because that's my time." Accordingly, the woman says she is able to relax and distance herself from her high-pressure days.

On the other hand, some successful women are happy because they have totally integrated their family life with their business life. Their children work with them in their businesses.

There are many different solutions to stress. What is important is that you find the one that is best for you. No one can decide for you. You must search your feelings and not allow yourself to be deterred from the course that is best for you.

You may find your life enriched by pursuing a variety of unrelated activities. A powerful woman who works in Washington, D.C., notes that she did. "Back in college I joined the board of the YWCA. I got on the board of a small chamber orchestra. I've always been a member of the Junior League and I do volunteer work." You will learn a variety of different lessons in different sectors of your life, which will help you through problems in other parts of your life.

Vacations are important. Some people deliberately seek out different challenges to face on their breaks. Trekking in Nepal, shooting the rapids in Idaho, scaling mountains in Tanzania to study the apes. Many people feel that by dealing with different unrelated stresses they clear their minds and return to their businesses refreshed and ready for the tamer stresses they encounter on a daily basis.

It's interesting to visit different cultures on your vacations. It helps you reevaluate the rules of the one you operate in. It can also make you more observant about this one. One of the advantages of exploring different areas on vacation is the perspective you get on the stresses of your work. These experiences can change you in some ways and solidify your values in others. Being aware that the Hopi Indians place no emphasis on physical beauty and that the Thais do not pick their neighborhoods according to money and status—this kind of information can stimulate creative minds.

If you are feeling stressed out and a vacation is imminent, postpone any showdown until after you return. You may discover that your fresh perspective enables you to smooth out what previously seemed to be an unsolvable situation.

You can also create mini-escapes for yourself. You take to the open road with your motorcycle and see things from a different vantage point. Or you plan a bike outing and picnic with friends. It's a complete change of pace. Rather than taking energy, these mini-escapes will create more energy to deal with the stresses in your life.

It is important that you not overlook the spiritual side of yourself. Spirituality is a kind of escape. Whether you meditate at home or light candles in a place of worship, don't neglect this important method of achieving inner peace and harmony. An hour of meditation can refresh and revitalize you.

Take advantage of the chapels in airports. Use them for quiet time. Step into a church between meetings. The minimum you will get is peace and quiet. The more stress you are under, the more important quiet, reflective time becomes.

One successful New York businesswoman meditates in the backseat of taxis as she rushes back and forth between meetings. "It refreshes me enormously," she comments. "It makes me more effective."

Do not hesitate to be religious. Many of the most successful people in our culture are candid about their intense religious orientation. It is a socially acceptable way of dealing with stress and coping with the problems of a complex business and personal life.

SCOLLARD'S LAW Escape is a state of mind.

FITNESS

Fitness is another way of taking a mini-vacation, of escaping from the daily stress you face. One woman jogs daily at dawn to solve problems. She jogs alone because she needs the "think time." She says that's when she does most of her problem solving for the day.

Find a sport for yourself that you enjoy and carve out time to pursue it. Exercise gives you energy. And energy helps you find a way out of seemingly impossible situations.

"Stress is something I live with twenty-four hours a day," says a corporate executive. "The only time I don't feel stress is when I'm exercising or when I'm on a ski slope. She has arranged for a physical instructor to come to her house four nights a week from 9:00 to 11 P.M. "We first walk four miles and then work out from there," she says. Moreover, she goes skiing every weekend she can possibly arrange.

Since we women are so busy, it is difficult to program fitness time into our lives. A professional painter exercises in the morning at six. One successful entrepreneur has a fitness instructor visit her at 7 A.M. every day. "It's my present to myself," she explains. The misery of my abdominal work is a welcome change from the stresses of my business. When I finish working out, I'm ready to take on the world."

If you feel great, you are less susceptible to being stressed out. Also, being fit reinforces your image as a confident, capable woman. People are more likely to trust you to get the job done if you exude vitality and energy.

One of the ways one woman rewards herself on the weekend and during vacations is by allotting more time to sports and exercise. Happiness for her is being able to work out several hours a day.

SCOLLARD'S LAW   It is easier to have a fit mind if you have a fit body for it to live in.

FRIENDSHIP

Friendship is one of the balms for the soul. A good friend who will let you pour out your troubles is a true oasis. Cultivate your friends. Don't neglect your friendships because of the other responsibilities and pressures that are on you at home and the office.

Women tell me, "I don't have time for friends." They are wrong. Of course they have time. It's simply a matter of setting their priorities. The wise woman puts her friendships high on her priority list.

A good friend will listen to your woes and then give you good counsel and advice. You can help each other through the minefields of living. Together you can avoid many of the mistakes you might otherwise make.

Choose your friends carefully. As a rule, it is wise to make your friendships outside of the office, keeping the two aspects of your life separate. This is particularly true if you own the business.

Generally your closest friends will be people who understand the stress and responsibilities you have as a risk taker. Ideally your friends will be risk takers themselves, people who have experienced many of the same challenges as yourself.

SCOLLARD'S LAW   Woman's best friend is not her dog.

7

Risk Strategies

JUST BECAUSE there is an element of danger involved in a venture does not mean that you have no control. You can take charge of your risks. You can limit the hazard to a level with which you are comfortable. Not only can you prepare yourself, you can also control many of the variables involved. First, we'll discuss some of the options available to you in risk taking. For instance, you can choose your risks, the size of the risk, its time, and you can use contacts and your political acumen to guide you.

Then we will analyze the different strategies you can implement to help you be successful. We'll examine what some other women have done. You'll discover that strategy is usually not as important as your innovativeness in playing with the cards life deals you. "Life lurches along," observes Boston psychiatrist Ralph Hirschowitz, adding that "luck and serendipity" have a lot to do with people's lives. They particularly do in women's lives. Our roles as mothers and wives greatly affect any strategy we may have had in mind when we started out.

YOU CAN CONTROL THE OUTCOME OF YOUR RISK TAKING

You don't need to approach risk taking in the same way you approached "Pin the Tail on the Donkey" when you were a child.

You don't have to be blindfolded anymore. You don't have to guess about where the back end of the donkey is.

This is real life and we're grown up. One of the advantages of being grown up, besides not having to drink your milk, is that you can take control of your life.

CHOICE OF RISKS

You are not at the mercy of circumstance. You can decide which risks you want to take. Of course, you must take some risks—not to risk is even a risk. But you can choose. Decide whether it is worth it to you to confront your boss on an explosive matter. Maybe it isn't. Think before you act. Evaluate your possible down-side risk versus your up-side returns. Analyze whether you are in a no-win situation. If so, walk away from it.

Of course, circumstances present you with an ever-changing variety of possible risks. For instance, you don't have to worry about whether to get married unless circumstances have dropped a very desirable man in your life. You don't have to worry about which of two jobs to take unless circumstances have created the possibilities.

You, of course, influence your circumstances. For instance, you may have contributed greatly to the presence of the gorgeous man who wants to marry you—you found him. Or the two jobs that are being offered you may have come about after some discreet and active politicking on your part.

But given the circumstances—however they came about—you can control the choices. For example, do you want to leave corporate life and start your own business? You should not rush to a conclusion. You should examine the possibility of the risk very carefully. Do you have the right mentality? Are you willing to work really hard? Do you have the discipline? Do you know that the marketplace is ready for your idea? Is the aggravation of running a business substantially less than that of employment?

These are some of the choices you can make. There are others: Do you want to have children? Do you want to make a lot of money? How hard do you want to work? Is your family your top priority?

Accept the fact that life does not dictate your choices. The ones you have available to you may surprise you—or dismay you—sometimes. But it is a mistake to relinquish control. You must be resolute about taking responsibility for the choices you make.

SCOLLARD'S LAW Be open to all the possible alternatives available to you in every situation. You can be very creative in your choice.

SIZE OF RISKS

You can also limit the size of whatever risk you choose to take. There are big ones and small ones. It's up to you. For example, doing your homework reduces the risk involved in starting your own business. If you have test-marketed the concept, lined up customers, and have money to spare, then your chances of succeeding are greatly enhanced.

Moreover, if you present a case for why you should be given a raise or promoted, your risk is minimal. If you threaten to quit if you don't get it, you've escalated your risks considerably. If you're setting aside $500 to test a business idea, it's a very different matter from gambling your entire $15,000 life savings.

Risks can have several different components. For instance, a job with a substantial salary increase in a new town may be a better risk than a dead-end job in the city where you are now. Relocating may seem risky. But dead-ending your career may ultimately cost you more. Refer to chapter 4, where we discuss at length how to accurately evaluate your risks.

You don't have to take giant steps. Risks can be taken in small steps. "I take risks the way I cut my hair—an inch at a time," says one entrepreneur. There is often little reason why you should lunge forward. Rather, you can feel your way. For instance, if you are starting a business, you can do as Flora Mattis did: She kept her full-time job and started her consulting business on the side, working several years during holidays, vacations, and weekends. After she had built up a base clientele, she quit her job and devoted all of her energy to what was already a thriving business. That was far less risky than if she had quit her job first and then looked for her first client.

Taking small steps requires patience. It means you move an inch at a time. But then, very few things require abrupt and massive commitments of time and money. Unless you are a seasoned business participant, it is difficult to handle abrupt surges in business growth. In your career and in your business you are far safer moving one step at a time—small steps.

SCOLLARD'S LAW   It is rare that you are forced to take a big risk instead of a small one.

TIMING

You can control the timing of your risks. Do you want to look for a new job this month? Or next year? Do you want to make a career change now? Or wait until the kids are out of college? Or out of grade school?

Timing is a key factor in success. It requires honesty and sensitivity. You have to be candid with yourself about where you are at a given time and what you want. And you have to be sensitive to your situation and the business climate. "I believe that there is a *right* time," says LaVerna Hayes, who quit her job and bought a skin-care business. "It's a major decision when you buy a business. It has to be right for you. My age was a factor. I was forty-two. I had wanted a business to nurture. If I don't do it now, I never will, I said." Her daughter was in college, and Hayes was burned out at the job she had, so she made the move. She's glad she did. Her performance at the salon is up 52 percent over last year.

Timing applies to entrepreneurship and it applies to any job. "I have a real need to continue to challenge myself. When it gets comfortable, I'm ready to move on," observes Ro Nita Hawes-Saunders, who owns a training and communications services firm in Ohio. Only she can sense that moment. It requires being in touch with herself and her environment.

Pam Fletcher-Hafemann observes that timing has to do with the success of a business, timing in both the business arena and in the personal life of the business person. "Timing is important in business opportunities. If you're the first with an idea in your area, your chance of success is greater." Indeed, businesses often have a moment when they are most viable. Sometimes it has to do with the costs at that moment. Sometimes it has to do with the mood of the marketplace, the pulse of the economy. It requires study and sensitivity on your part to discern the "right" moment. It has to be the right time for you also. "If I had started this business when the kids were two and three years old, it might have been much harder," notes Fletcher-Hafemann, who opened her own full-service beauty salon when the kids were teenagers.

"Timing is important as far as *you* are concerned, too. It has to do with what you want at different stages of your life. I wouldn't have done this fifteen years ago. I didn't have the confidence or the background," says Fletcher-Hafemann.

Another woman, who is now self-employed, recalls how she became sensitive to new opportunities when she was in her early forties. "You go through many stages in your life when it's time to move on, and you have to recognize when it's time to move on," she says.

Sometimes you have to wait for the right time. "It took me five or six years to make the move, to get a divorce, to move on. Everything in life is timing. You do it when you're ready," notes another successful risk taker. "It takes a while to work on it, but when you do, whatever you want is there."

It is difficult to try to force the right time. If you're not ready or the marketplace is not ready, it is far easier to fail when you take a risk. Roxandra Antoniadis, a New York school admissions director who has had a varied and successful career, says she is very sensitive to the right time for decision making. "I don't ever force decisions. If you don't know what to do, keep living one day at a time. The process of living will provide you with the answer," she notes. "The risk lies in waiting for the moment to come when you know what to do. It takes faith in yourself to wait for that moment." It is important not to buckle in to pressure to make a decision. "Never make a decision because everyone is on your back pressuring you to decide," advises Antoniadis. "Never force a decision."

The time in your life is an important factor in making successful career moves. There are preliminary moves you must make in order to gather the experience and confidence to be prepared to make certain others. When you are just starting off your career, learning is more important than earning. Usually when you're younger, you are able to live on less money and have more energy to pour into a job than later in your career. "I don't have the energy," declares a *now* successful executive who started off her career working eighteen-hour days for several years.

With women, our families are always a critical aspect of the timing of our career moves. When we have young children, they require so much energy that it may be a time when we want a less-demanding career. If we get married, we will want more leisure time to spend with our husbands. It would be the wrong moment to take on a job that requires working seven days a week.

SCOLLARD'S LAW   Our intuition is an important asset when it comes to determining the right moment to make a move.

CONTACTS AND POLITICS

When you are dealing with an established business, you must be sensitive to the politics of everyday corporate life. You need to be aware of who makes decisions and how the decision process works. If you are in a political structure, you have to be attuned to the mood of the decision makers and how they can be persuaded to give you whatever it is you want. Contacts within the power structure can be of great assistance, clueing you in to the climate and the most effective procedures.

Ideally, before you deal with a power structure, you should

learn about it so that you never have to go in "cold." Knowing the right person can be invaluable. Says an experienced corporate executive, "When I'm ready to make a move and I want to join a certain organization, I call on a mentor to help me scope it out—who I need to talk to, who should call up and promote me at that organization. In Washington, you don't need to know how to do things as long as you know someone who does."

Cultivate your contacts. They're the closest thing you can find to the old-boy network.

SCOLLARD'S LAW Only political creatures thrive in established power structures. If you're not political, stay with small organizations.

SOME THINGS YOU CAN CONTROL

Just because strategies frequently go up in smoke does not mean that you must relinquish all hope of ever having control. There are variables you can control. It is important to nail down all the things you can so that you are best situated to deal with the changes life will bring.

For one thing, you can usually control the number of risks you have to take at any given time. If you're getting an unforeseen divorce, don't voluntarily take a number of other risks simultaneously. Keep your job. Don't move. Don't have another child until the divorce is over. *Then* face your next risk.

It is important that you *not cluster your risks* so that you can give each your undivided attention. If you are maneuvering through a tricky business situation, keep your family life stable.

Do not ever voluntarily change everything at once. If you're getting married, wait six months before you look for a new job. If you are getting a divorce, wait a year before you quit your job and start your own business.

Generally you'll make better judgments if you are able to give each situation your undivided attention.

Length of Jobs. Unless you get fired, you can control the length of time you spend at your job. It is important not to stay too long. For one thing, women frequently encounter discrimination, and it is necessary to move to another company in order to move up. Don't blind yourself to the situation. When you are hindered, move to another company where you can move up a rung. If necessary, move again in two or three years.

Another mistake women frequently make is staying too long in one job. Women are noted for being loyal employees. Sometimes that loyalty can prompt them to stay too long. As a rule of thumb, you should always think about your next job whenever you take a new job. You should network to increase your visibility and increase the opportunities of being offered other jobs. You should be friendly with at least one very discreet headhunter.

Usually, after a promotion from staff to management, you should move. If you were somebody's assistant, some people in that organization are going to continue to treat you like somebody's assistant, no matter how capable a manager you are. Create a new environment where your new persona can flourish. Move to a new company where they've only known you as a manager. You'll get more respect.

If you find yourself in a difficult, nonsupportive corporate situation where you can't get as much of a raise as you want, negotiate a new, more powerful title. Be very tough in the negotiation. Act like you will never leave. Then take the title and market yourself for a bigger job elsewhere.

When you get a big raise or promotion, don't feel *grateful.* You deserve it. Women still have to work harder than men to prove ourselves. When you get a big raise, you should be wondering how much you're worth to the competition. If you're so valuable, are you worth even more across the street?

Be particularly alert to changes taking place in your company and industry. "The hot spots change every few years. There are constant changes," notes Alicia Fox, a sales executive with the

ABC-TV network in New York. She says that people are generally well advised to change jobs every four to five years. Of course, if you're moving to be in the "hot spot," you're going to be in the limelight. That added attention should pay off in raises and promotions.

SCOLLARD'S LAW   Sensational careers result from sensational career management.

The Right School—The Right Degree. One asset you can bring to the marketplace is the right college degree. Frequently an MBA is a woman's way of making a statement about being serious. Although the jury is out as to how much an MBA helps your career in the long term, it is certain that an MBA never hurts. One woman earned an MBA just to underscore her seriousness. It did not. "I think it helped my résumé," she says. "It also helped people's perception of me. I don't need it so much now as when I was twenty-five just so as not to be perceived as a puffball. I definitely think had I been a man, I wouldn't have bothered," she adds.

Sometimes the school you pick for college turns out to be an advantage. "Going to Yale was a tremendous asset," notes one woman. Generally if your college is going to be an asset, it helps only for the first few years of your career. After you are thirty, your performance is a far more important barometer than where you went to school. After you're forty, your college degree becomes irrelevant.

SCOLLARD'S LAW   If you have to choose between another degree and relevant work experience, go for the experience.

Beginnings. Although you can't control the outcome of your strategy, you *can* control the beginning of it. If you want to be in a certain field, study the various methods of entry. If you are young, don't be proud. Enter wherever you can to get the job you someday aspire to. If you are older, your choices may be more limited. A forty-year-old woman working in the typing pool is perceived very differently from a twenty-year-old. Do not fool yourself about your prospects. Analyze what's going on in a company and figure out how to get where you want. Analyze how your superiors perceive you. Perception is important.

In beginnings, every option is available to you. Take full advantage of the opportunities. You can get a great deal more experience working in a small company than a large one. Judith Moncrieff, now an executive in corporate America, recommends that when you first begin, you would do very well indeed to have your first couple of jobs in small companies. "You'll get more experience," Moncrieff notes. "You'll get more responsibility." Of course, working for small businesses is riskier. Generally they don't pay severance. The pay may be lower. But it's much harder to work up in a big company than in a small one. You have less visibility. "Gain as much experience as you can on the outside," advises Moncrieff, who has worked a decade at a $50 billion-a-year company. "Enter into a big corporation from as high a point as possible."

Big corporations offer certain advantages. Generally you work fewer eighteen-hour days and there is more stability. And there is room for substantial growth and promotions. A big corporation is a great place to learn formal management skills that will stand you in good stead should you decide to leave and start your own business. Moreover, the *benefits* a big company can afford are wonderful.

But generally speaking, you will find the excitement and the growth opportunities in smaller companies. Never limit yourself. Once you've done a good job in one area, branch out into new ones. If you've developed a good reputation, you may find you are frequently considered for exciting new positions. Don't ever do the same thing day after day—unless it turns you on.

SCOLLARD'S LAW Consider new beginnings at several different points in your career.

Goals. Having doubts about your ability to take risks successfully does not mean you should not set goals. It's essential to have objectives. Having a clear view of your goals makes it easier to assign priorities and thus easier to make decisions when you face a fork in the road. It's important for you to have a clear understanding of whether or not you want to start your own business. It's essential to know you want to avoid the bureaucracy of corporate America and want to work solely for smaller companies. It's important to decide whether you want to make a great deal of money at any price.

Don't be inflexible about your objectives. As you change and life changes, your objectives may change, too. Leave yourself open. "I always sit back and say, 'If I were being interviewed when I'm one hundred years old for *Time* magazine, what are the most important things I would want people to remember me for?' " asks a successful entrepreneur. "I start there and I play these mind games and go through goal setting. Every five years I go through goal setting." She says she has met all of her current goals, so she's in the process of setting new ones.

Prepare yourself as much as you can to meet your goals and accomplish your risk taking successfully. A woman whose goal was to be the first woman in the management hierarchy at a stodgy male company consulted with an attorney about how precisely she should subtly remind her boss of the need of the company to promote a qualified woman to its upper ranks. Thoroughly prepared and well rehearsed, she handled herself wonderfully in the critical interview for a management position. And she got the job.

Once you have set your goals, use them as a device to force you to focus your life. Keep your goals in mind. Don't waste your energy running in circles when you could be pursuing a goal. Once you set your goal, every step should be in that direction. Otherwise you may find yourself going in circles.

Some of the most successful people have always been goal oriented. They learned to set them at an early age and continue to redefine them as they grow. "I've been deliberately setting my goals all of my life," notes a successful executive.

Don't narrow your horizons deliberately just because your goals are well defined. Leave yourself open to changing your mind. Life is long and interesting, and you shouldn't eliminate too many possibilities. Don't close doors unless you have to.

SCOLLARD'S LAW   There is a Chinese saying, "Door close. Window open."

Excellence. Your own performance is one of the few things you can continually control. You will find that your reputation is your greatest single asset, particularly as you grow older.

One of the fascinating things about business is that each industry is so small and word travels so quickly. Your integrity and superior performance are quickly known in your industry. Value your good name. Do your best to protect it.

Everyone pays lip service to wanting to get ahead, but only a handful are willing to take the effort to distinguish themselves with the extra effort and an extra degree of excellence. You need to understand that dues have to be paid. And when you are paying them, pouring your best energy into whatever task is necessary is how your reputation begins to be made.

Even in major corporations, your performance is more important than your political acumen. "Your performance guarantees your longevity," notes corporate executive Judith Moncrieff. She tells her staff, "Make me look good. Save me from myself." If you do this for your boss, you are necessary to your boss. Regardless of personal prejudice, you are likely to keep your job.

SCOLLARD'S LAW   There is no substitute for excellence.

DIFFERENT STRATEGIES AT DIFFERENT TIMES IN YOUR LIFE

The plans, objectives, and strategies you employ should reflect where you are in your life.

Your Twenties. Use your early years to explore, to learn about the world, and to take inordinate risks. Don't worry about how things are going to look on your résumé. Take unusual opportunities and unusual risks and learn what your capabilities are. By the time you are in your midtwenties, you should be getting a feeling for what your strengths are and what you enjoy doing.

Don't worry about breaking rules. If you get a disastrous job, quit soon and find another one. If you get a better offer, take it. If someone wants you to move to another city for an exciting opportunity, move. Take full advantage of your flexibility and your youth. By the time you are in your late twenties, you should have found a direction that appeals to you and should be working twenty-three hours a day to prove yourself.

Your Thirties. You may find a job satisfaction in your thirties that is emotionally fulfilling. You learn that you do indeed have valuable skills. You've learned to manage yourself and you're learning to manage other people, too. "Emotional fulfillment replaces the sexual fulfillment in your twenties," notes ABC salesperson Alicia Fox.

You should have settled into a career path and be able to demand greater salary increases. As the intense energy of your twenties is running out of steam, you should be learning to delegate and motivate other people to produce for you. It's now time to think about titles and to consciously expand your portfolio.

Your Forties. The entry-level jobs that looked cute when you were twenty-five are no longer appropriate when you are forty. If you are returning to the job force, consider two things: Go to work for a small business where the managerial skills you used to manage a household can be appreciated and put to good use. Traditional corporate America does not recognize any experience except the type that men typically have amassed.

Or, if you can't find the right small business to work for, start your own. By the time you are in your forties, you know how to get things done.

In your forties you have proved yourself, learned to manage yourself, and learned to manage other people. If you are working in corporate America, it is during this period that you should consciously expand your authority and look for opportunities to demonstrate your ability to deliver.

This may be about the time when you realize that you are dead-ended in your career. It is the period during which many women take the business and life experience they've accumulated and decide to start their own businesses.

Your Fifties. By this time in your life you should have found a secure niche for yourself. If you don't like what you are doing, you should drastically reassess your life and start doing what pleases you.

If you are in corporate America, you have probably been promoted as far as you are going to go. If you don't like your job, consider a dramatic life-style change.

This is a decade when, if you have not done so before, you should indulge yourself. Do what makes you happy. Some women opt for early retirement. Others opt for part-time work. Still others are still attacking their careers with as much energy as they did in their thirties. Don't apologize for what makes you happy. By this age, hopefully, you have learned to be your own person.

Your Sixties and Beyond. Your sixties are no longer considered to be declining years, but instead they are vital and full of opportunity. If you are in corporate America, rules are rules, and you're probably being nudged out into retirement. The question is whether or not you want to retire. It's a personal matter. One of the great things about being in your sixties is that there is less pressure on you to conform to people's expectations. People don't have rigid expectations about how you should perform at this age, as they did when you were in your thirties and forties. You are as free to explore the world as you were in your twenties.

Take full advantage of the freedom available to you. You can work full-time, start your own business, take on different kinds of jobs to learn about the world—it's up to you. There are few rules. You get to write your own.

And there is history to be written as women in their sixties, seventies, and eighties revitalize and revise society's expectations of this period in a woman's life.

SCOLLARD'S LAW   Our expectations for our sixties, seventies, and eighties are undergoing a dramatic shift. There are exciting opportunities for us to explore all the possibilities available now.

CAREER STRATEGIES

You hear a lot of hoopla about the importance of career planning. To emphasize plans and goals is frequently a waste of time. Those plans and strategies are often useless. The world changes. You change. Your family changes. Often these changes are in absolutely unforeseen ways—marriages, divorces, industries hitting the doldrums. The world is a very interesting and unstable place.

Study the paths of the careers given in these pages for examples. Note how people's lives change. How could Roxandra Antoniadis, for instance, have planned her life when she had a life-threatening illness that forced her to resign from teaching. Thus she was thwarted in the job market in the late 1970s, when academia had a serious glut of teachers, and was forced to reconsider her career. How could she have foreseen those events or planned for them?

Consider Alicia Fox: She did not even expect to have a career. And once she had one, how could she have foreseen that she would marry and that that relationship would be the dominant force in her life? Only Judith Moncrieff and Ro Nita Hawes-Saunders, of the examples given, were able to implement career strategies that seemed planned and logical.

Not only are we affected by unforeseen shifts in the economy, we are far more impacted by changes in our personal lives. That's why a woman's family status is noted at the top of each of the case histories that follow. Having children makes a difference in our career decisions. Being a single parent, getting married, getting divorced—these can be important factors in our career decisions. Pam Fletcher-Hafemann waited until the children were older before she started her own business. One of the factors in Ro Nita

Hawes-Saunders's decision to start her own business was her young daughter. Being an entrepreneur gives her increased flexibility to meet her family's needs while maintaining high professional standards.

Because the best-laid plans are frequently for naught, flexibility and creativity are important ingredients of success. When we roll with the punches, there are many opportunities to be original in our choices.

If you feel comfortable having plans in place, make a series of contingency plans. Have plan A, B, C, and D. It is easier to land on your feet if you have previously considered having your well-thought-out plans upset.

Better yet, instead of spending your time making plans, you would be wise to study the dynamics of the world around you and consider at length the variables that could occur. Frequently things change so quickly that you have little time or energy for planning. You make snap judgments to cope with a shifting universe.

Gathered together here are outlines of a few women's careers. All of these women are happy, well-adjusted people, pleased with their lives at this point. But note how different their career paths have been.

When you study these profiles, pay special attention to the following matters:

- Information is included here you would never find—or want to use—in a résumé: personal information. Getting married, divorced, raising children alone—these are all factors in the choices women make in their careers.

- If you read between the lines, you can see that frequently a major career decision was made for unplanned reasons—a marriage, a divorce, a death, children. Women do not have the luxury of focusing solely on their careers, as men do.

- Note where women started off. Frequently it was in a different direction from where they're headed now.

SCOLLARD'S LAW Women's lives are far more interesting than men's.

SCOLLARD'S LAW You need a clear view of your priorities while you're rolling with the punches.

CAREER STRATEGY:
From Being an Employee to Being on the Fast Track as an Entrepreneur

---

Pam Fletcher-Hafemann, age thirty-eight
Single mother of teenaged boy and girl
Owner: Images Unlimited, a full-service beauty salon
          Seventeen full-time employees, six part-time
Parents couldn't afford to send her to school. After high school, went to beauty school in order to qualify for a job that would enable her to work her way through regular college. Initial ambition: To be a teacher.
Won competition in beauty school. The prize was a job.

1968–1976	Worked as hairdresser in two different salons. Worked her way through college. Married. Had children.
1976–1979	No traditional teaching jobs available. Taught in beauty school. ("I learned the insides of the beauty business.")
1979–1985	Divorced. Needed more money. Relocated and went to work at prestigious LaCosta Spa in California. Because of her teaching background, was soon made directress of skin care. Was there six years. ("I loved it. It gave me credentials, confidence, and contacts.") Remarried.
1985–present	Saw need for a salon that supplied beauty services similar to those at the spa for the average person. Saw opportunity in the booming southern California marketplace. Found a financial partner.

Opened her own salon in 1985. (Divorced again in 1988. Compares her business to marriage: "It's like having a love affair with your work. The minute people fall out of love with a business, it falls apart.") She loves it. She feels she's found her niche.

CAREER STRATEGY:
Steady Success in Corporate America

Judith Moncrieff, age thirty-seven
Married.   Manager, Research and Production, Mobil Corporation
       Seven staff people

Graduated with honors in political science from Hollins College. Worked one summer at the National Municipal League. A professor arranged for her to interview with them for a full-time job when she graduated, which she got.

1972–1974	Editor and columnist, National Municipal League.
1974–1976	Director and editor, Features Department, *The Wall Street Transcript*. Moncrieff couldn't make ends meet on the salary she was making, so she sought out a part-time evening job at the *Transcript* to supplement her meager salary. She worked until 6:00 P.M. at one job, from 7:00 P.M. until 11:00 P.M. at the other. Within a few months the *Transcript* offered her a full-time job. ("I was working twelve to eighteen hours a day. It meant giving up my social life. But it was the best learning experience I ever had.") She reported directly to the publisher, "a stern taskmaster."
1976–1978	Chief editor and writer, L. F. Rothschild, Unterberg, Towbin, an old-guard Wall Street firm. ("Working for a small business on Wall Street,

to get a promotion, you have to move.") She was still working twelve to eighteen-hour days. ("You're either learning more or you're earning more. Early on I opted for learning more. I was building credentials, picking up knowledge that prepared me for my next job.")

1978–present   Moncrieff was ready to move from the Wall Street side to the corporate arena. She went in as an investor relations adviser, representing Mobil and talking to Wall Street. She later moved into her current job as an in-house advertising manager. During the decade her salary, rank, and portfolio base have increased. She administers a $6-million budget. (Working in a large, male-dominated corporation requires political acumen and sensitivity, but "your performance is more important than politics.")

CAREER STRATEGY:
"Fun" Beginning, "Serious" After Thirty, Marriage Comes First After Forty

---

Alicia Fox, age fifty-one
Married.   Sells daytime program advertising for ABC-TV network

Fox was brought up as a product of the gender gap. ("Men knew they were going to be breadwinners from the moment they were born. A woman expected *maybe* to have a career. We were brought up to fill our time with work. I never expected to have a career.") Graduated from the University of Miami. ("I filled up my time with work. I was not serious. I was enjoying life.")

First job—   Then PR for a hotel chain. ("I got to travel be-
receptionist   tween Fort Lauderdale and the Bahamas.") Then a brief stint as an interior designer in California. A brief marriage. Then fund raiser for the Ameri-

can Cancer Society. ("Now I'm twenty-eight years old. I'm beginning to start thinking.") Then assistant manager of PR for El Al. Another "fun job"—but more responsibility.

1968–1973   Takes cut in pay for three months to prove herself at a "serious" job. ("I'm close to thirty.") Director of client relations, ABC Sports, New York

Gives herself a four-year plan to prepare for career job. Targets sales. ABC has no training program. Fox trains herself on vacation time. Persists.

1973–present   Daytime programming sales. She's happy there. Intends to stay until she retires. ("They say you give 50 percent to the office and 50 percent to your husband," says Fox, who married Michael Wynn at age forty-one. "It doesn't work that way." She estimates she gives 30 percent to the office and 70 percent to her husband. "I'm extremely happy in both aspects of my life.")

CAREER STRATEGY:
Active Seeker of New
Challenges

Ro Nita Hawes-Saunders, age thirty-seven
Married. Mother of two-year-old daughter
Owner: Hawes-Saunders and Associates, which provides professional development training and communications services

When she was a teenager, she wanted to be an actress. Her first paying job was in a summer-theater program at the age of fourteen. ("I learned that you could take something fun and get paid for it.") In college one of her summer jobs was working as a long-distance operator—something she did not think was fun. ("I wasn't going to be doing it forever, and it gave me skills I could use during Christmas.") While she was in college, she traveled to New York to investigate acting. She learned that she was not willing to make all the necessary sacrifices. She went to graduate school to study broadcast journalism, working at a public television station part-time.

1974–1976	Assistant Director of community services at a broadcast station. She achieved her first goal: to have her own show.
1976–1982	Volunteered at a local public TV station and was hired as a producer. ("After two years in any job I'm ready to move on.") She stayed at the station but she was promoted three times.
1982–1985	Director of news services, University of Dayton. (This gave her an opportunity "to learn about politics.")
1985–1987	Supervisor of marketing and media services, Dayton Board of Education.
1987–present	("I've had great fun. I enjoyed every job," she declares. "But I decided I didn't want to work for anyone else.") Plus Hawes-Saunders now has a young daughter to consider. She is pursuing an application to own a radio station in a nearby suburb.

CAREER STRATEGY:
Two Different Careers End Up As One

Roxandra Antoniadis, age fifty
Single parent, two children
Marketing and Admissions Director, St. Hilda's & St. Hugh's School, an elite private school in New York City
The daughter of a diplomatic career officer, Antoniadis was raised in Brazil, Germany, Switzerland, and Holland. She majored in French at Connecticut College and began teaching it at age seven-

teen. When she finished school in 1959, she "didn't want to be a secretary and wait for a husband." She decided to take advantage of the six languages she spoke. ("What do I have to offer? Who would want what I can do?") She approached the Executive Council of the Episcopal Church to give her a job—she taught herself to type just in case. They offered her a job in Japan. She took it.

1959–1961	Teacher, Japanese Episcopal College.
1961–1966	Returned to school to work on Ph.D. program in French at the University of Colorado. Taught as associate.
1966–1968	Got married. Taught full-time. Finished dissertation for degree. ("My son was born twelve hours after I turned my dissertation in.")
1968–1977	Assistant professor, Miami University, Ohio. Got divorced in 1974 with children ages four and six.
1977	Suffered from life-threatening illness. Forced to resign her post. Recovers. Sends out two hundred résumés. No teaching jobs anywhere. Spends a month visiting her mother and job hunting in New York City. ("I stayed on the phone. I got a job.")
1977	Researcher, Episcopal Church.
1978–1980	Director of Resources Development, Episcopal Agency. Works in public relations and volunteer programs.
1980–1986	Antoniadis decides to take her public relations skills into the business world. ("I looked at me. I looked at the market.") Lands job with perhaps the most prestigious public relations firm in the country, working for Letitia Baldrige. Within three months is account executive. Becomes vice president.
1986–1988	Antoniadis goes out on her own. Takes on glamorous clients, such as the prince of Lichtenstein.

1988   Antoniadis finds opportunity to marry her educa-
        tion and public relations skills working for elite
        private school in New York City. ("I was looking
        for an opportunity like this. After I had formu-
        lated in my mind exactly what I was looking for,
        I found it.") Stay tuned.

CAREER STRATEGY:
From Housewife to
Restaurateur

Rosemary Garbett, age fifty-two
Widowed mother of four
Owner: Los Tios Mexican Restaurants
         Ten restaurants, 375 employees
Garbett married at eighteen against her father's wishes. She never
went to college, staying home to raise her four children. ("We
lived on $100 a week. Living on a budget is very much like
running a business.") When she was twenty-eight, she was too
insecure to fill out a form at a class reunion.

1970   Her husband started one restaurant. She worked
        wherever he needed her. ("I was a very domina-
        ted housewife.") She worked as a cashier and
        kept the books.

1976   After opening their third restaurant, her hus-
        band died—with no insurance. The kids were
        aged between thirteen and nineteen. ("I had to
        feed them. And I had to prove I wasn't just a
        housewife.") Suppliers and employees doubted
        her abilities; she had to pay them in cash. Her
        accountant and attorney advised her to sell. She
        fired them and kept the business. Employees
        quit. ("I set out to prove them all wrong.")
        Garbett is now one of the most recognized
        business people in Houston. She is diversifying

her business to include food production for other Texas restaurants and is selling products to a grocery chain. Moreover, Garbett has not borrowed money from a bank since 1977—her expansion has been financed out of her profits. ("I was a survivor then and I'm a survivor now," declares Garbett. "Everyday is a learning experience.")

CAREER STRATEGY:
From Social Butterfly to Successful Entrepreneur

Tina Z. Potter, age thirty-seven
Widowed
Owner: Tina Z. Potter & Associates, Inc., International Communications

Potter was an underachiever in a privileged overachieving family. ("I never made over twenty in math in high school. I didn't care.") After going to boarding school in Switzerland, she failed her SATs and was barely admitted to the University of Texas, where she majored in languages. ("I skipped classes to be social and to sunbathe.")

1973–1978	Fashion buyer for a large department store. ("I was ahead of myself. I could spot trends.") When she quit that job, she was in desperate need of cash. The day she was going to apply for a job as a cocktail waitress, she received a call offering her a job as merchandising director for a Beverly Hills store. She accepted.
1978–1982	Decided she would be better off self-employed, so founded a fashion consulting and public relations firm with a partner. She met and married John Potter, a successful attorney and former judge. They were head-over-heels in love.

1983–present   Five months after they married, he died. ("I grew up quickly.") She bought out her partner and moved into an office so small there was no room for visitors to sit. She took an idea her husband had the night before his death to start a calendar-of-events book, *The Black Book*. ("I learned I needed credibility. Through persistence I gained it.") Potter made *The Black Book* a substantial financial success and sold it in 1988. Now she has a varied list of international clients. Potter, who routinely flunked math as a child, now does her own financial projections and is a dedicated busi-nesswoman. ("I've always been a dreamer.") Pot-ter still has a dream: "I'm going to be a tycoon," she vows.

CAREER STRATEGY:
From Journalist to Corporate Manager

Merry Clark, age thirty-eight
Single
Director, Editorial Projects, Hearst Corporation
Clark grew up in Austin, Texas, and graduated from the University of Texas, where she was a popular, achieving student. "Women were taught they would be married." She was—for two years in the early 1970s. She worked at the *Harrisburg Patriot News* and went to school at night to earn an advanced journalism degree.

1975–1978   *New York* magazine
               Clark got a divorce and moved to New York with no job but several friends. Through her network she was offered a job at *New York* magazine, writing a popular column.
1978–1979   *Cue*, New York. The magazine folded.
1979–1981   *Miami* magazine.

1982–present   Got a job at King Features division of Hearst as editor of *Sunday Woman Plus*. Took a national syndicated weekly supplement, doubled its client list, and it grew tremendously, working with two hundred free-lance writers. She was recognized as management material and was the only woman promoted into management. ("Careful risk taking is an important part of corporate life. You have to take risks to be successful in a company. If you think you can be narrowly focused and get promoted, you are wrong. Women are afraid. I've been pushed to the wall and had to fight back. Pick your battles. Never be petty. Only fight back when it's important. Get the right allies. Fight the right battle. Use the right language, and have one sport that you really know a lot about." Clark grins about how she was recently described by a colleague: " 'Brilliant, beautiful, and has a mouth.' You notice they said 'brilliant' first," she points out.)

CAREER STRATEGY:
Tired of Making Money for Other People, Makes It for Herself

LaVerna Hayes, age forty-three
Married, one daughter in college
Owner: Interlude Skin Care Center, complete beauty services, Dayton, Ohio

Hayes finished high school expecting to be a housewife. Married with a small daughter.

1970   She looks for part-time work. Goes to work for Hot Sam's Pretzel Co., one of a chain of fast-food outlets then owned by General Host.

Made up her mind she wanted to be manager. In six months she convinced them she could. ("It got me out of the house.") She planned her hours around her daughter's school schedule. She worked at "being the best manager in the company." She was. Her store was the top producer in the company, which owned four to five hundred outlets. Hayes collected bonuses and benefits. ("I received every plaque they knew how to give—number-one everything. They all knew who LaVerna was.") There was no place to go. ("They were promoting the men, but not the women.") She burned out. ("If I don't start my own business now, I'll never start it.") She did.

FLOWING WITH THE RIVER

When you put together your résumé for perusal by the casual observer, you put the best face on things. You never mention your personal life. All you talk about is business.

But that isn't the way things really happen. You may have plans and strategies and objectives, but a woman's life is influenced by other-than-business factors. Frequently the neat, tidy résumé you see is the product of a woman creatively meeting the risks and challenges of her business life and personal life and having scrambled successfully to make the most of it. "I used to waste a lot of energy trying to change things, to make them fit my goals and plans," notes a successful entrepreneur. "It has been a lot easier since I learned to roll with the punches and flow with the river. There's no point in trying to change what happens. I finally learned to simply make the most of the moment instead of trying to change everything.

Becky Tedesco, now a successful entrepreneur in Washington, D.C., recounts the circuitous path from her childhood to her current ownership of a thriving temporary service. "Money or business success was not something that counted in my household. It all came about accidentally. I started as a schoolteacher. As the result of a divorce I then became a sales representative for Xerox. That's where I had my first taste of how to be a salesperson. It just evolved from that. When I moved to Washington, I became a stockbroker. Not because I wanted to be, but because I was a single mother with a child to feed, and it was the only job that I went on an interview for where they were going to pay me for six months to study. I didn't want to be a stockbroker, but I was smart enough to realize I needed a paycheck to support my child." Tedesco accidentally discovered the employment business, too. "I knew the day I got into it that this is where I wanted to be."

Tedesco, using her intuition and courage, trusted her instincts and has grown enormously in the business she ultimately discovered.

Harriett Berman, who runs a retail store in California, was motivated by a divorce to start it. "Not much planning went into starting this business," she admits readily. "Once we got the idea, my friend Helen and I got started within a week. It was not thought out—it was just timing. We started out with very little money. All the labor was our own. But we did business from day one. All our business is word-of-mouth, no advertising, the location and our merchandise." Berman is an example of how women use their intuitive skills to launch themselves in business and how capable we are of learning as we go.

Asa Miller learned about business when her husband became very ill and she had to step in and take over the reins for him. "I proved to myself I could do it after a traumatic experience of almost losing my husband and having to run the business so that it would be there when he got back. It was a scary time for me."

Maybe Miller was scared. But she was certainly competent. And very much in the tradition of women stepping in when there is an emergency and doing whatever is necessary to survive.

Says Berman, the retailer, "The options are there. It's scary, because you don't know that they are—but they are. You just have to keep your eyes open, and when the opportunity arises, you have to take it and not be afraid, because the worst thing that can happen is you don't make it and you go on to something else."

These women have figured out an exciting way to achieve success—they keep their eyes open, propelled usually by necessity rather than by ambition—and apply their survival skills to business.

Life is so dynamic and filled with unexpected developments and opportunities that we women may be at an advantage. Well educated, with a new business orientation, we are well situated to grab the opportunities as they arise. We are well positioned to deal with the dynamics of a fast-paced twenty-first-century life.

Now that we have business goals and have accepted the reality of needing to work in a business world, we are in a unique position to move creatively and quickly.

SCOLLARD'S LAW   Women have always had to cope with adversity and the unexpected. It's finally beginning to pay off for us in business.

HIDDEN AGENDAS

You can be very private about your hopes and goals. One woman confides a hidden agenda she has composed for herself. She has realized the importance of focusing on one risk at a time and paces the risks in her life. Last year her risk was having some plastic surgery done. This year it was a promotion. Next year she intends to look for a job at another company. The following year she hopes to get pregnant.

SCOLLARD'S LAW   You can achieve almost everything you want to. But not probably on any kind of schedule. Accomplish a goal when the opportunity arises. Forget the time frame.

HOW TO MINIMIZE YOUR RISKS

1. Be patient. Don't rush into a risk.
2. Stall until you *feel* ready.
3. Research the outcome as much as possible before you venture forth.
4. Do not make a decision unless you feel calm and centered.
5. Be brutal in analyzing the Worst Possible Case. Could you live with it?
6. Be realistic in your expectations.
7. Every risk has a "right" moment. Use your intuition to find it.
8. Once you make up your mind, go for it. Don't back out until you have given your risk a chance.
9. Take a series of smaller risks.
10. Once you venture forth, pay attention to all the little things that happen.

A CHECKLIST FOR YOUR STRATEGY

1. Does it incorporate your goals?
2. Does it take your age into account?
3. Are there alternatives at every point of the way? Are some of the alternatives attractive to you?
4. Are essential points of your strategy things you can control?
5. Do you have the contacts to make it work? Do you know how you will make the right contacts?

6. Are your risks spaced out? Will you have time to prepare for each one well in advance?
7. Are you comfortable with the risks you need to make?
8. Does your strategy reflect your personality?
9. Is your personal life factored in?
10. Is your strategy aggressive enough? Don't be afraid to aim high.

Risks and Your Love Life

ONE OF THE INTERESTING ASPECTS of women who take risks in their careers is that they have also dealt with risks in their marriages. Therefore they have previously considered at length the status of their relationships with the men in their lives. They have carefully evaluated their relationships and made appropriate judgments about these men. Unlike many women, risk takers tolerate little middle ground. They either have excellent relationships with their husbands and lovers or they have dismissed them from their lives.

They have carefully weighed the effectiveness of their relationships, because to become a successful risk taker, they have had to formulate a clear view of themselves and their priorities. This includes their relationship with the men in their lives.

While risk taking may be a major preoccupation, ideally it should not overwhelm your life. After all, the object of risk taking is to enhance the quality of your entire existence. Success at business is part of a whole life and not everything in itself. A round and full life entails success on a broader scale, both business and personal. Frequently that includes having a special man.

Some women disagree. Some women insist that they find enough intensity and self-validation in their business careers to satisfy them.

Some parts of life are negotiable for many women. Men: perhaps yes, perhaps no. Children: perhaps yes, perhaps no. But risk taking and success: definitely yes: No *ifs*, *buts*, or *maybes*. The self-actualization that accompanies risk taking is central to a woman's sense of identity and personal growth. Husbands and children cannot substitute for your own personal self-discovery.

Another interesting thought to consider: Would a book about risk taking written mainly for men include a chapter about women? Probably not. Why? That's probably the difference between being a wife and being a husband. It doesn't come up as a factor in a man's career because he doesn't have the burden of the relationship. The wife does. He's the husband; he doesn't.

Husbands and children are still primarily a wife's responsibility. Since we are the wives, they are factors to consider in addition to our business careers. We tend to accept the responsibility of our children. But an unsupportive, difficult husband, that's another matter. Him we can do without.

But you can have it all. It's up to you to design your life so that you fit it all in. Marriage and successful risk taking frequently go hand in hand.

In this chapter we'll discuss all the different possibilities of relationships successful women risk takers formulate with men. We'll consider the full range, from women who consider husbands to be merely a disposable commodity, to women who believe it's only natural to be single, to women who are devoted wives.

SCOLLARD'S LAW   There's no such thing as a typical marriage.

MARRIAGE AND SUCCESS: You Can Have Them Both

The secrets of being happily married and successful are not very different for risk takers than they are for everyone else. What differs is that the intensity is often far greater. Happy marriages of risk takers and their men have the following ingredients.

Growing Together. In any marriage it is important that people grow together, but if one-half of the couple is a woman who is stretching her capabilities by taking risks, a woman who is constantly challenging herself and expanding her limitations, it means that the husband has got to be doing the same thing if he is going to keep up, says sixty-one-year-old stockbroker Nancy Blanchet, who is not married.

To grow together, you've both got to have similar capabilities. Adds Blanchet, "If both are capable of personal growth, then they'll grow together and grow stronger. If one is a dud, then that one's going to be a dud regardless."

As a risk taker you very likely will equate your personal growth with your risk-taking success, so any man who holds you back will be regarded as being anti-you. Then problems arise. You must understand that it is unlikely that the two of you will grow at a similar pace. Usually each of you grows in spurts, with one moving ahead and then the other one taking the lead. "It's very rare that you grow laterally with the same person all the time," observes a woman who has been married for thirty years.

As you are both growing, of course, your relationship is changing to reflect the changes in both of you. The relationship shifts. To continue to stay married, you must both be satisfied with what the relationship becomes.

"My marriage goes through a lot of changes, just like I do," says a woman who has also been married for many years. "I don't know that I'm not going to meet someone to sweep me off my feet, no matter how strong my marriage is. Maybe something might happen. My husband's a physician, and there are a lot of nurses. How do you know nothing is going to happen? Things change because of the growth and exposure you have in the world outside of your marriage. You have this growth when you're out and you're learning all the time."

Any marriage has to be strong enough to withstand the fact that most successful couples experience totally different universes when they leave their home and go to their careers. They're each meeting new people, forming new relationships, entering new competitions, and making new friends. Unless the relationship is cemented together, it is easy to be critical of the spouse or of the nature of the relationship. People were far less critical of their relationships a hundred years ago, when they were exposed to only a few others for comparisons. Today, when you are in a different city every few days, encountering literally hundreds of new people each week, that gives you an enormous basis for comparison.

If you are both growing, it is important not to be unduly harsh on each other or the relationship whenever you see something that looks better from your vantage point. One thing is sure, marriages present a public face that frequently has little to do with their reality. Often the most perfect-appearing relationship is only a facade behind which lies a wasteland.

If one of you stops growing while the other one is a star in the stratosphere and reaching farther still, you must each come to terms with the differences in your life-styles if the relationship is to continue. The star must not be condescending, and the one who stopped growing must not be jealous of the attention and success the other one gets. It can be done. But traditionally it is men who have been the star and not the woman. It takes a remarkably secure man to bask in the reflected glory from his wife.

SCOLLARD'S LAW When you are growing and taking personal risks, you are usually risking your marriage, too.

Balancing Act. In successful marriages there is a constant fine-tuning taking place. You're constantly communicating with each other about your changing priorities and adapting to each other. Your priorities do change. They shift constantly, and this puts strain on your relationship.

Notes a financial executive, "What happens to the young woman is that she gets a job. And then she gets a husband, and she can still manage that—it's not too big a problem. Then they have children, and all of a sudden their priorities are all shaken up. So they have to readjust their priorities in midstream."

Women have the most difficulty with the balancing act because the main weight of the problems is still on their shoulders. We are bombarded by images of superwoman: being a wonderful mother, a seductive wife, and a fantastic businesswoman. We have to juggle those priorities, ideally in unison with our husbands. It isn't easy.

Then there's the problem of balancing our objectives. If you're in the midst of a demanding challenge that requires seven-days-a-week work for six months, and your husband wants to retire and go fishing, it is a serious problem. Notes one woman, "My husband is at a point in life where he's taking more time off from work and thinking of retiring and he's coming to realize that I need to get out and do my own thing. It's difficult because it's a transitional period. He was used to me being at home and being traditional. Now that I have my own fabulous business, I'm not ready even to think about slowing down. So it's hard for him. And the roles are reversed at this point. We're working on it."

You usually need to balance the intensity of your ambition so that you are in sync. Notes an independent television producer, "In marriages, if you have somebody who has no ambition and somebody who has lots of ambition and one holds the other back, it's not going to work. If you live in two different leagues, there's no interest."

Both of you can be intensely ambitious, but if one of you enjoys great success while the other fails, it creates an imbalance in the relationship. One woman still bemoans the end of what had been a perfect relationship to a man whose career was going great guns when they first married. Once she got serious about her career, she became one of the most successful women in her business. "Unfortunately his was zagging down as my career was zigging up. It created enormous emotional battles," she recalls. She blames the failure of the marriage on the fact that this imbalance was never rectified: Her career continued full speed ahead while his crumbled.

It is possible for an unambitious man to live with a woman who is intensely so, but it is usually simpler if they were that way when they met. Several successful risk takers have confided that they prefer a husband who is noncompetitive and who has few ambitions. One woman has such a live-in lover, who is delighted both by her ambition and by his total lack of it. When asked what he does, the man, who does not work at all, merely replies, "I don't work. Ask her what she does. She does it all." Why not? Men have been married to wives who felt that way for years. The older generation of women routinely answered inquiries about their identities with the answer of whom they were married to.

For some of the new kinds of relationships to work, men are having to liberate themselves from the traditional macho male hang-ups. Hopefully we'll continue to see more and more successful relationships that were previously considered to be unorthodox. As we women explore options for ourselves, we have to be open to expanding the options available for men in our society.

SCOLLARD'S LAW   We will have completed the great Equal Rights Movement of the twentieth century only when both sexes have the same life-style options available and can choose them without being the subject of scorn or curiosity.

Conciliations. You can have been married for years and think you see eye to eye until you see a risk-taking opportunity and go for it. You succeed. You get hooked. The old status quo of your life becomes unacceptable. It seems to your husband that overnight you're a different woman. Whether he likes the new model more or less is a major factor in the success of the marriage.

And the question we always have to ask ourselves as wives is how much we are willing to give up for the marriage.

Traditionally we gave up whatever was necessary to maintain the relationship. If we were married to a man who moved fifteen times in twenty years, we moved cheerfully along, keeping safe, flexible jobs as teachers and secretaries, which were available anywhere. We never had a career on track because that was sacrificed. There was one career in the family—his. That has changed. Risk taking is exciting, and we women like doing it, too. Also, we need our own economic platform: Marriage is no longer "forever." It would be very uncomfortable today to rely totally on a husband for your economic well-being.

But now what do you decide to do if one of you needs to make an important career move—to another city? Or if one of you wants to slow down and move to the country? How are these decisions made? Not easily.

The glib and easy solution touted in the 1970s was that you both do your own thing. At that time we heard a lot about couples who lived in different cities and commuted—the best of both worlds for each of them. Maybe so, but it was tough on the marriage. Not a single one I am personally acquainted with survived. The sole remaining bicoastal couple I knew sadly divorced last year.

The solution of the 1990s is far different. Whatever you choose, if you value the marriage, one of you will make substantial concessions. The solution of Jan Duval is a harbinger of what couples of the 1990s will do. She married a man in Dayton, Ohio, while she was working for Reagan at the White House. They commuted. "It was difficult," she recalls. "I wanted to live with him. Parts of me were burned out. I wanted to see what it would be like to live with my husband." They both changed their lives. Her husband took a job in New York, and she made a midstream career change and moved there, too, where they now live together.

Marriage for risk takers requires creative solutions to succeed. The advantage you have in finding solutions for your marriage is your flexibility and imagination. These traits will enable you to design your lives so that both of you will be happy and the marriage will survive.

SCOLLARD'S LAW   Your career should not be your only priority. Love is important, too.

Common Ground. You and your mate should have common interests to sustain the marriage. At your work each of you may have your own universe of people and ideas, but when you are together, it is important that you share certain activities. Frequently one of you enjoys an activity more than the other, and one of you compromises to make the other happy and to share the experience. For instance, one couple who have separate, high-powered jobs in very different industries and businesses continually accommodate each other in sports and hobbies. She wasn't thrilled about it, but she trekked with him to a fishing outpost and learned to catch trout—because fishing is one of his great passions. He wasn't thrilled about it, but he took painting classes with her—and found that he's very talented and enjoys it very much. They've taken cooking classes together, which he enjoys more than she does. And he's learned to love her dogs, which were once far more important to her.

This couple has a very successful marriage because they are constantly exploring the world together, discovering each other's joys, and sharing them. At the same time they have substantially enhanced both of their lives. She is now at home in hip boots in a stream, and paintings by both of them are on display around the house.

With all the pressures of their careers pulling them apart, they have solidified the relationship over a decade of marriage by expanding the things they have in common.

SCOLLARD'S LAW You and your mate must go out of your way to cultivate each other's interests, or your lives may become so separate that there is no reason why you should be together.

Respect. In addition to self-esteem a successful marriage also contains mutual esteem. You value the person you live with, the risks they take, and the successes they achieve. You want to be taken seriously.

It's easy to become frustrated if your husband takes your efforts lightly. Comments such as "Why do you bother to work, honey, if that's all the money you're making?" can be demoralizing. "After taxes, transportation, paying for my work wardrobe, and the baby-sitters, I only net $50 a week," says one woman, who went back to work after becoming bored as a full-time wife and mother. "He doesn't understand how much what I accomplish means to me. I'd work if I didn't earn anything at all. My work makes me feel good about myself." The lack of respect for her labor is a source of friction in the marriage. She takes very personally his lack of respect.

Another housewife who got a job encountered the opposite reaction. "My husband respects me more for it, even though he has to do things for himself I used to do for him. I think men and women respect you more when you work in business. More than when you're just doing benefits. More than when you volunteer."

A Midwestern housewife who returned to work over her husband's protests says, "Women have to fight for recognition, to be taken seriously. A lot of hard work at your job can break your marriage or strengthen it. There are a lot of broken homes."

When you work and take risks, the center of your world shifts further away from your husband as you focus your energy on achieving success. By the same token, you can't expect him always to be taking care of you. He's out there taking risks, too. You have to respect his endeavors, even if that means he sometimes neglects you. "Don't get upset when your husband forgets to send you flowers or whatever," advises a public relations expert. "Just do it yourself."

You respect each other's preoccupation with your jobs and become perhaps more direct in your communication with each other. If it's your anniversary and you think he's going to forget and it's important to you that he remember, remind him. Remind him several times. Make whatever plans you want made, and remind him of them so that he doesn't forget.

Mutual esteem means that neither of you expects the other to sit around reading the other's mind. Be forthright. You're both too involved with the various risks you are taking to devote time to trying in vain to read each other's mind. If something is meaningful or important to you, say it. Don't wait for your spouse to guess, and if he doesn't, don't punish him.

SCOLLARD'S LAW   Risk taking changes your priorities. The day may come when you'd rather celebrate your latest success than your own birthday.

Personal Growth. Within the context of the marriage there has to be room for you to explore yourself, to discover what you can be, and exactly how much you can do. Ideally the growth of one of you should stimulate the development of the other. Marriage becomes like a basketball game: You and your spouse are a team, passing the ball back and forth. You achieve common goals and yet both are able to develop themselves.

Says Gale Lee Gilbert of her decision to cease being a full-time housewife and start her own limousine business, "Doing something like this has added to our personal growth and has made some very big changes in our lives."

Accepting those changes requires patience and flexibility. Nothing can stay the way it used to be. Everything moves forward and becomes slightly—or dramatically—different. When a housewife becomes an entrepreneur, the relationship with her husband becomes substantially different.

You have to permit each other space to grow and take risks. Moreover, you must support each other during the difficult phases and accommodate each other's changes by changing your self and your demands.

SCOLLARD'S LAW To grow, you must permit each other plenty of space.

Time Alone. You should arrange your life so that you have two kinds of time alone: by yourself and with your husband.

Time by yourself is invaluable. You must leave space for each other to spend time alone. To think. To focus. To plan and create. This time is often one of the first things that a busy risk taker foregoes. But to give this up is a mistake. If you feel harried, strung out, overworked, and overstressed, very often the solution is to give yourself time every day to focus your thoughts and to reach for an inner balance.

Most healthy relationships require that you also plan time alone together. Not just when you sleep together at night, but active waking time. You need romantic time and time just to focus on each other and talk about incidental things.

With the pressures of children, friends, and business entertaining it is easy to find that your time is constantly spent with other people surrounding you and your mate. To avoid this situation, you need to set some rules for time together. Reserve either certain nights of the week or part of the weekend for just the two of you. One couple allocated every Sunday for themselves. It is the rule and not the exception that they have a quiet day alone together, not initiating any phone calls and accepting no invitations. Without this deliberately arranged togetherness they feel that the pressure and pace of their lives might cause them to drift apart.

It is easy to get so caught up in everyone else's affairs that you sacrifice your personal time and damage your closest relationship. Beware of this. While you are planning your life and calculating the risks you are going to take, factor this time into the equation. When you are setting your priorities, this should stay high on your list.

SCOLLARD'S LAW   It takes a hands-on approach to time management to guarantee that you'll be able to have time on your hands.

RISK TAKING CAN ENDANGER MARRIAGE

As we have seen, marriage and risk taking are not mutually exclusive for many successful women. However, this is very individual. Some women say they just do not have the knack for having both. Says a very successful businesswoman, "I tried. But I couldn't juggle all the balls, so I let the other areas of my life go while I concentrated on making the business work. Those are the risks you have to take. And I lost my family because of it." While remorseful, she would not do it differently if she had it to do over again.

Success is addictive. The thrill of risking and winning is intoxicating. In comparison, the thrill of a marriage is quite tame to many women. Some women say they tried to manage both areas of their lives. When push came to shove, the husband and the marriage seemed less central to their identity. So the marriage became history.

Another woman says that her marriage was fine as long as she worked at menial jobs and earned little money. The problems only began after she started making a lot of money—which ironically she was only motivated to do because she wanted to be able to afford a maid. "My husband thought it was good I had a job. But he didn't think it was good I was making money. He was very threatened. When I got serious about making money, I made two-thirds as much as what he was making. He hadn't minded my working until I became successful." Later, under pressure to give up her job, she divorced him instead.

That was the case with Becky Tedesco. She is quite candid about what occurred in her marriage as her temporary service business was being built. "I didn't know how to jump in and allocate my time and keep a personal life going at the same time a business life was going on. I'm amazed and always fond of anybody who could do that. But I don't lie when they ask me. My answer is, 'No, I couldn't,' " she says. The effects were substantial. "It disrupted my entire life."

A West Coast executive agrees with Tedesco. "There's no way to balance your professional life with your family life," she insists. "There's no way to be successful in your job and do the rest correctly. There's no way to balance it. It's impossible." In her effort to deal with the stress of the two commitments, which to her were in direct conflict, this West Coast woman spent five months in a hospital recovering from drug addiction problems. "There's no question that my job ruined my marriage. There's no question about that."

There is also no question about what this woman's priorities were. When the job and the marriage were in conflict, she let the marriage go. It is important that we all take responsibility for the choices we make in our lives. Having to choose between a husband and a business life is an undesirable situation to be in. If we love both facets of our lives, it is always possible to resolve the two. It's a matter of recognizing and accommodating your priorities.

Some women have little conflict when push comes to shove.

Declares one woman, "My personal growth is more important than any husband. I collect husbands and I have outgrown them all. Husbands just level out into comfort zones, where they love the status quo. They just love it. They were taught somewhere along the way that they just go from step A to step B to step C and then you stay there and you've got it made. So they stay there and they level off. Well, if I keep growing and he levels off and stays there, he looks like a jerk."

When we consider marriages that have ostensibly been destroyed by women's successful careers, it's important to consider one other thing. There is a question as to how solid, how satisfying, how good a marriage it was anyway. Admits one woman who used to blame the failure of her marriage on the pressures of her corporate executive life, "I now believe something that I didn't accept four years ago. I believe that our marriage would have cracked, with or without the career. Because if it wasn't strong enough to withstand a difference in my life-style, how strong was it? I wasn't screwing around. I wasn't drinking. I wasn't using drugs. The only thing that was different was that I was working and becoming successful. If the relationship wasn't capable of surviving that rubber-band pull, then it probably would have collapsed anyway. I tend to blame it on my career. To make it my responsibility." She says that now she realizes that she has accepted the guilt unnecessarily. "There must have been problems that I didn't acknowledge before I started working. I was going bonkers staying home. One of the reasons I went out to build a business life for myself was because there were already problems in my marriage."

The question really becomes: How little are we willing to settle for? The answer is: Not as little as before. In past generations women sat home and silently endured lousy marriages with little else in their lives to give them a sense of pride and identity. Now women have the option of discovering themselves in business life, too. Risk taking is thrilling, and the sense of yourself you gain doing it is intense and gratifying. What is happening is that when a marriage fails, it's no longer the end of the world, particularly if you already have a separate world of work that provides satisfactions of its own. The ideal may be, for some women, to have both marriage and a successful business life. But there seems to be a consensus that if for some reason the two cannot coexist, it is simpler to find another husband—or to do without altogether—than it is to chuck your career. And I wonder, is it possible for a woman of the twenty-first century to dump her career to keep her marriage and be happier than if she had done the opposite?

But isn't it a matter of priorities? And is it fair to assume that whenever there is a conflict between your risk taking and your marriage, the marriage is automatically the less worthy of the two? Could it be that the marriages that are abandoned may have been weaker marriages than the ones that survive?

As a rule of thumb, I suggest that you continually evaluate the quality of your marriage and the suitability of your mate along with the level of intensity of your career. You should make every attempt to avoid deceiving yourself about the quality of either aspect of your life.

One woman says she was building her career and simply taking her husband for granted. And he was just the kind of husband that she wanted. She ignored him to the extent that the relationship was in jeopardy. After a stormy scene she realized that all she had to do to salvage her relationship was pay some attention to him, to make even a small effort to be nice, to go a little out of her way to let him know she cared. She did. Now she has both a successful career and a happy marriage.

Which brings us to an important point: Don't drive your husband or lover out of your life unless you're sure you prefer it without him. If he's truly important to you, there's almost always a middle ground you can find where both of you are content.

If you care deeply about the man in your life, there will be a way you can negotiate a balance between the demands he makes on you and the demands of success. If push comes to shove, you may decide to give less to your job and more to him.

SCOLLARD'S LAW   It's up to you. You can have a career. You can have a husband. And, if you're willing to compromise, you can have both.

A DIVORCE CAN BE A
LAUNCHPAD TO SUCCESS

Some women are able to turn unpleasant events, such as divorce, into a positive incentive to take risks, explore the world and themselves, and become successful. Divorce, a traumatic and unpleasant occurrence, actually becomes a positive time in their lives. There can be three different ways that divorce can be positive.

Making the Most of a
Difficult Situation

Some women are so strong that they manage to make something positive out of any difficult situation. They take the cards life deals them and play the best hand they can. For them, divorce is usually not something they desired but something that happened. One woman, whose husband unexpectedly left her to marry another woman, says, "My neck was broken in an automobile accident when I was twenty-two years old. I thought that was the most difficult time of my life until my husband surprised me a week before Christmas with the news that he was in love with another woman. I was stunned. This divorce and my broken neck were the two worst things that I have ever been through. And they have turned out to be two of the best things that ever happened to me. They both changed my life for the better, and I'm a far better and stronger person because of these events." This woman was spurred on to take new risks and start new ventures by her divorce. "I've done things, started businesses, I never would have done if I hadn't been dumped," she reports.

A Midwestern woman, a housewife during her thirty-five years of marriage, was also abandoned by her husband. As she recovered from the shock, prompted by the necessity to support herself, she hocked her engagement ring and purchased a convection oven. She now has a prosperous baking operation. Another woman found herself divorced with two small boys, no skills to get a job, and a nice car. She made the best out of what she had and now has a thriving limousine company in Michigan.

We women are a resourceful lot. We have the tradition of centuries of women being promised the world by men and then being deserted by them. Women have often found tremendous inner strength and discovered aspects of themselves they never would have known had adversity not struck.

Says a Washington, D.C., woman, "My divorce was the best thing that ever happened to me because it made me grow up very quickly. I had to look into money. Before, I had put myself in a situation where I didn't have to make choices about money. Now I may end up by myself," says the woman, who has since remarried, "but now I'll be alone with room service. I can afford it."

Often women who dedicate substantial time to their husband's career, entertaining, and being the traditional "good wife," giving generously of their time to *his* career, find themselves freed up to pursue their own interests once they are a solo act. A Virginia-based woman, a housewife before her divorce, found herself needing income to support her two small sons. She turned the artistic skills she had used decoratively around the house to become the basis of a new business, painting canvas rugs that are sold in museums. Had it not been for her divorce, she very likely would never have explored that aspect of herself. She says she is far happier with herself now than when she was married.

Women who made the most out of a difficult marriage are nice people to know. They are not complainers. They are doers. They are not victims. They are survivors. They always land on their feet. They have resilience and imagination. They have accepted the fact that we live in a less-than-perfect world. You will rarely hear them complain. They are busy discovering what is possible within their given limits. When the rules change, they change. They are adaptive and usually very positive human beings. Risk taking comes easily for them because they have confronted unexpected challenges. The fear of the unknown is lessened as they cope with the unexpected and win.

SCOLLARD'S LAW   Some people crumble under adversity. Others build marvelous new structures out of the rubble of their lives.

Freed by Lack of a Husband

Some marriages are confining and restricting for women. Some husbands are terrified their wives will leave them if they discover their own capability and success. These husbands are a strong negative influence in their wives' lives, deterring forward progress. It is as though the man feels that if the wife was able to make it on her own, she would leave him.

Sometimes the worst fears of a confining husband are well justified. Wives do leave men like this and strike out on their own to take risks and explore their capabilities. Says Patricia Harrison, "My divorce allowed me to do things on my own time in my own way without explaining why I was doing the things I was doing. Someone got out of my way. Did me a favor and got out of the way."

Says Sally Marshall, "My life didn't blossom as a professional woman until I got a divorce. I used to direct everything that was happening to his life. When I did work, I didn't feel that I got his support."

A prominent Washington, D.C.–based stockbroker agrees. "When I started my career, I did it in order to see if I could afford to get a divorce. Then the first year it became obvious I could do it, so I got a divorce and continued." She says the freedom of a divorce left her more able to deal with the two-pronged priorities of being a career person and a mother. "I had chucked the husband, so that was no longer a problem," she chuckles.

Some women free themselves from the shackles of a confining husband. A generation ago they might have persevered in the marriage, suffering silently. No more. More and more women are insisting on the freedom to discover themselves and grow personally. The reason they talk about their careers blossoming after they leave their husbands is that they find that personal growth and the risk taking of business are inexorably intertwined. A husband who blocks their career is essentially blocking their development as a human being.

SCOLLARD'S LAW   Nothing takes the bloom off the rose of marriage as thoroughly as a husband denying a wife the opportunity to blossom.

Becoming Another Person

Sometimes the trauma of a divorce forces a woman to redefine herself and become a different woman. It is painful. But the result is similar to the phoenix rising from the ashes. The woman becomes a different, much stronger woman than she ever envisioned she could be.

Nancy Helmer says, "My divorce was the best and worst thing that ever happened in my life. It made me do a lot of growing. I think when you go through something like a divorce, it forces you to do a lot of growing. For me, in my late thirties, it forced me to evaluate my values. Were they my values or values others had given me? I've reevaluated everything, and what I am now I'm a lot more comfortable with. It's more me. The divorce gave me freedom to be really happy and do what I wanted."

Another woman says the process was slow because she was so insecure during and after her marriage. "It took years before I could see my way," she reports.

Reconstituting yourself after a failed marriage can be painful and may take a while. It takes determination and persistence to make yourself the person you want to be—but these are the same characteristics that are so essential to successful risk taking in business. "I was such a basket case in my marriage that when I looked in a mirror, I honestly couldn't see myself," confides one Colorado-based woman. "It took years before I looked in the mirror and saw anything I liked. Now when I see myself, I'm very pleased."

SCOLLARD'S LAW There is no one to blame for what you are except yourself. You must accept responsibility for what you make of yourself.

A GOOD MAN IS A GOOD SUPPORT SYSTEM

At the other end of the spectrum, some men are incredibly supportive of the women in their lives, contributing ideas and encouragement to their success. These men cheer their women on, saying, "Go for it. You can do it. Life isn't any good if you don't try new challenges." If you have a man like this in your life, your risk-taking process is certainly likely to be achieved with considerably less pain and struggle.

What motivated attorney Dona Kahn to leave her job and start her own firm? "I think my husband did. He said, 'Why are you talking about it. Why don't you sit down and figure out what you need.' He focused us in on what we needed in order to take the plunge. And we decided it was something we wanted to do—and why not?"

Says Debbie McAteer about her business, "My husband is very involved. Always cheering me on, asking me questions. When we met, I was going through a recession in my business and feeling depressed. He'd sit down with me in meetings and just kept saying, 'What can we do to make it better? What can we do to improve this?' He really had a lot to do with the business succeeding after that."

Christine Dolan says her boyfriend has been a "100 percent motivating factor" in the forming of her own TV production company. "It was he who was the catalyst for getting me to the point of saying, 'Hey, let's play in the big leagues,' " she reports.

If you have a man in your life who encourages you to take risks and seek greater success, listen to him. Remember that a husband or lover who believes in you is a blessing. Take it and go forward.

SCOLLARD'S LAW If you have a man who believes in you, do him a favor and believe in yourself. Go for it.

SCOLLARD'S LAW Should you fail, being comforted in loving arms is a great consolation.

SCOLLARD'S LAW A good man is hard to find.

LOVE AND BUSINESS CAN INTERTWINE

Some of the most intense and satisfying relationships between men and women occur when they are not only lovers but business partners as well. Pillow talk is business talk. "We even discuss business when we shower together in the mornings," says a woman who is in the publishing business with her husband.

The relationship is intense because unlike other two-career marriages, where you enter separate worlds when you part company in the mornings, you live parallel lives. Your togetherness is profoundly together. You problem-solve together and interact in each other's lives twenty-four hours a day.

Patricia Harrison founded a business fifteen years ago with her husband and one secretary. Now they have built a Washington, D.C.–based business with forty employees in Washington and eight people in Dallas. She says, "The business is part of our lives. If I have to travel or he has to travel, I think there's more understanding because we both really know what it takes and how exhausting it can be. It's not one person doing something and the other person trying to explain why I can't go with you or why I can't take you, or what I can't anything. We do things very, very independently, but together where it counts." Harrison and her husband started off working closely together, but as the business has grown, she says, "It's large enough that we don't even see each other during the day. I never even think of myself as working with him. But it's fabulous. We always have something to talk about."

Says Christine Dolan, who works on a one-on-one relationship with her boyfriend, "Doing it alone isn't as much fun. Two heads are better than one. It's important to me that he and I go into business together for personal as well as professional reasons. The professional reasons are it's a great mixture. It's going to work whether or not our personal relationship survives." Incidentally, Dolan says business partnerships are easier for her than the emotional aspect. "What was risky for me was going from the *I* to the *we.* Part of that is surrendering, but it's surrendering to a 'we.' There's more to gain and more to lose."

Photographer Carol Highsmith notes that her work is now a shared effort. "I used to work around the clock and was only accountable to myself. Now my husband is sucked into it, too. So now it's the two of us. We're working on the books together. We are both *living* the books right now."

The involvement, satisfaction, joys, and difficulties that you share in a marriage-business partnership are extraordinary. If these relationships survive, they are a work of art. If these relationships fail, the acrimony is frequently even more intense. Not only does the marriage end in divorce, but often there's a business divorce, too.

SCOLLARD'S LAW Don't fear sharing your entire life with the man you love. The chances for failure in marriage-business partnerships are no greater than in any other marriage.

SECRETS TO SUCCESSFUL BUSINESS–MARRIAGE PARTNERSHIPS

Complementary skills
Clearly defined roles
Separate roles

When disagreeing, walk away from the project
Always putting the marriage as the number-one priority; the
business is number two
Not second-guessing each other
Backing each other up
Sharing each other's successes
Sharing responsibility for failure
Similar objectives
Similar energy levels
Great communication skills
Devotion
Can-do personalities
Attitude of forgiveness
Willingness to admit to failure
Willingness to turn a task over to mate when encountering
difficulty
Honesty about shortcomings

HOW TO KEEP LOVE ALIVE WHEN YOU'RE UNDER PRESSURE

I consulted a happily married couple to discover their secrets for sustaining a remarkably congenial relationship despite the fact that they both have high-pressure careers. She is Judith Jones and she has a successful catering firm in New York City. Her husband, Dan Ambrosini, is a union organizer. They have been married for fourteen years. Here are some of their tips for happiness:

1. Ask for your mate's opinion. Respect what he has to say. Let him know that you respect his opinion.
2. Go out to dinner. Get out of the stress environment. Then discuss it.
3. Use your mate as a sounding board when you are contemplating taking a risk.

4. Share the excitement. Sometimes at night Jones talks about her business for hours.

5. Support each other in nonwork-related projects. Jones, who says she is shy, recited some poetry she had written in a poetry competition. She won, and they gave her a certificate. Ambrosini declared, "They didn't give you enough," and surprised her by giving her a huge trophy he had had made up for her.

6. Keep your sense of humor. Help each other when one of you loses perspective.

7. Agree on goals. Involve each other in decisions. Before Jones takes on a particularly demanding project, she discusses it with Ambrosini.

8. Call each other just to say, "I love you."

9. Know each other's eccentricities.

10. Help each other however you can. When Jones is particularly tired, her husband massages her feet at night before she goes to sleep.

11. Countdown to keep your perspective. When Jones is overseeing a large event, she says, "Tomorrow it's all over." As it approaches, she tells her husband, "In six hours this is history." Then they celebrate after the event has been a success.

12. Reinforce each other. Says Ambrosini, "She tells me how great I'm going to be. She compliments me. Makes me feel wonderful. On the other hand, she helps me. If I don't dress right, she tells me, 'That shirt talks louder than you.' "

13. Take care of each other's problems. Do what you can to make life easier for each other when one is under particular stress.

14. Don't unnecessarily burden each other. "We don't have to be nice to each other's friends," says Ambrosini.

REGRETS

No matter which decision you make about business, you may likely have regrets. Unfortunately, there is no perfect course to choose, and whichever way you go, you may sometimes consider what would have happened if you had done things differently.

Some women who have placed their careers over their marriages later have misgivings. Says television executive Lynn Loring, "Sacrificing my marriage was not worth this. I think women who become extremely successful in their chosen field have made almost a conscious choice to give up one to have the other. To give up the wonderful home life to have a business life."

Another West Coast woman agrees with Loring and says she would rather have a good marriage than her career. "If I were madly in love with a man who said to me, 'I really want you to give up your career so that we can travel and be together,' I certainly would," she declares.

Other women have none of those misgivings. They only wish they had given up their marriages sooner and gotten a head start in their careers.

A Midwest-based executive urges women not to hesitate to put their career first. "Had I started when I first felt like it and not subjugated myself to a man and been a wife, God knows what I could be doing now," she says.

Opinions about the relative value of marriage and work vary from woman to woman. It is important that you form your own, remembering that how you arrange your priorities is as personal as your signature.

SCOLLARD'S LAW   Regrets are a waste of time.

SCOLLARD'S LAW   When you make decisions about your life, try to predict that you will have no regrets down the road.

LOVE TAKES A BACKSEAT TO BUSINESS

You may find the risk taking in your business life so rewarding and so exciting that you may need little else in your life to make you fulfilled. Because of the satisfaction and reinforcement you get from succeeding in your work, you may decide that it takes preference over any relationship.

Both men and women make this type of voluntary sacrifice. Says Michael Linder, producer of *America's Most Wanted*, "I've sacrificed relationships. I left my lover back in Tokyo and I maintain a long-distance relationship with phone calls and letters and a lot of trust. The sacrifice is not living together day by day." He feels there is an impasse in the relationship because if she were to move to the United States, "I can see the inevitable resentments, the inevitable 'I've sacrificed my life for the sake of your career' type of arguments. I don't want that for either of us." But with his career booming here, it's unlikely that he would move there either.

It's a matter of priorities, and even though it may make us sad, we often favor our business over the men in our lives. Says Sally Marshall, "I wish I could spend more time with the man in my life. Instead I sacrifice my time with him."

Observes a successful West Coast woman, "Now, first and foremost, my life seems to be more focused on the business world, and my personal life takes a backseat. I am not unhappy about that."

Some women have difficulty finding a balance between business and romance. Says a woman who has built a sizable company, "People who are compulsive don't know balance. The real fire burners—the Type As—they don't know balance. They see only one thing and they go for that thing. Everything else is neglected along the way. They simply don't know balance."

Indeed, some people become obsessed in their business, neglecting not only the men in their lives but their friends as well. One woman sadly admitted that her business growth has cost her not only the men in her life but most of her friendships with women as well.

Some women opt for singlehood, preferring the simplicity of their lives. They view husbands as simply one more responsibility—one that they are happier without.

A successful stockbroker says that her life is easier now that her children are grown and she is unmarried. "My career took off more when all the kids left home, because I now work a full day and my mind isn't distracted. I mean, nobody has the measles. Also being single is a lot easier. You don't have to rush home and cook dinner for anybody."

Some jobs are so draining you understand that being single is part of the qualification for the job. Jobs requiring incessant travel or strenuous labor or excessively long hours almost preclude having any relationship. You simply lack the time or the energy any romantic relationship requires. Says Jan Duval of her term as production manager to the President in the White House, "In jobs like that, you need to be single. I worked every Saturday. I could never go anywhere for the weekend. I wanted to sleep all weekend. It took a lot out of me."

It's important that you honestly evaluate the demands a risk will put on you and weigh the commitment required against your other priorities. If you are young and single and eager for the experience of an incredibly demanding job, there is little reason not to go for it. But if you are involved in a relationship that is important to you, you must carefully weigh the consequences of risks that would lead you to intense demands on your time. If you value the relationship, you can make decisions about your risk taking that will protect it. The choices are all yours. There is no one to blame but yourself.

It is difficult sometimes to be married and successful at the same time, observes psychologist Jacqueline D. Goodchilds. "One of the things that is changing is that women work and marriages don't. So there's a lot of change. The notion that people go through life coupled is not the way it happens for most people in our society. It's either sequential types of relationships or a lot of people choosing singlehood."

The entire range of options is available, from singlehood to placing your relationship over your business. There's no one who can tell you what to do. It's up to you. You must look within yourself and see what is important.

SCOLLARD'S LAW   If your career is the most important thing to you right now, don't apologize. If your man is the most important thing in your life, don't apologize.

SCOLLARD'S LAW   The order of your priorities today is one thing. Next week you have every right to change your mind.

FOREVER WIFELESS

We must compensate for the biggest liability we'll ever have in our business careers—we'll never have a wife. We *are* the wives.

In addition to our businesses we also have the lion's share of responsibilities for our husbands and children. The total burden can be great. "All of us need wives. Not old-fashioned husbands. We need someone to take care of things," comments a corporate executive.

Because of all the responsibilities that we have, we're less likely to tolerate the demands of an old-fashioned husband. They must accustom themselves to fast-food takeout and laundries that deliver. It's an extra strain on a relationship if your husband is demanding and refuses to accept responsibility for a substantial part of the household—in addition to taking care of most of his own needs. "When my husband tells me his shirt is missing a button, I tell him where to find a needle and thread," comments one executive.

In short, a love life has a much better chance of survival if the husband or lover carries his own weight. If he caters to you as much as you cater to him. If he accepts his role as a true equal in the household. If he treats you with some of the niceties of life women have traditionally done for men, such as ironing your blouse in the morning while you bone up for an important meeting or forgoing his golf on Saturday morning to wait for the repairman to fix the freezer.

Busy risk takers are formulating less-traditional styles of relationships. In the absence of having a wife, the traditional so-called wifely duties are being divided up and done for each other.

SCOLLARD'S LAW   A husband who performs some wifely chores for you is preferable to being single. Life is easier.

SEPARATE IDENTITY

You may choose to be married to someone, but you're certainly not content to be Mrs. John Doe. In the last generation, women routinely identified themselves as an extension of their husbands. "My name is Mary Smith. My husband's a doctor." "My name is Jane Doe. My husband runs the hardware store."

These days are long gone. We've taken the responsibility of creating our own identity. Marriage is only comfortable if it permits you to develop your sense of yourself.

Men don't necessarily like it when their previously full-time wives establish their own careers and identities. Notes one woman who began a now-successful business after her children were grown, "Suddenly I'm going back to work and it threatens his life-style. It can be very threatening to a marriage. One no longer has the need to hold on to that one person, and other people are attracted to you when you become successful. When you have your own identity, you develop confidence. It gives you leverage. You have more freedom. It makes you feel like you're not dependent on someone else for psychological or financial support. It gives you confidence in meeting people and making it on your own. It makes you independent."

Problems arise in a marriage when a husband hinders a woman in her search for her own identity. And women hesitate to enter new relationships for fear that their separate identity will be blurred. "There are times I think to myself, 'God, it would be nice to be taken care of,' " admits an executive. However, she continues, "I have never had to look to anyone else for my identity, and for that I am grateful."

SCOLLARD'S LAW There's no reason why there can't be room for two very separate identities in one marriage.

FIRST SUCCEED, THEN
FALL IN LOVE

It's increasingly common for women to first concentrate on personal growth and success before entering into a long-term loving commitment. Without the personal growth that comes from risk taking and exploring themselves, there is no point in forming a relationship.

"I think a person has to be growing, and that's the most important thing to do before you have a relationship," notes a successful entrepreneur. "Once you have achieved personal growth and you're open to continue, then you can have a relationship and not before. If your personal growth is stunted, you can never have a successful relationship. You can never be happy with yourself.

"I want to have a family and a successful business," she continues. "I want it all and I see it happening simultaneously. The business has already happened, and now I'm working on the personal life. Now I'm going to spend more time on my personal life. Once I have that up to speed, hopefully the two aspects of my life will run simultaneously."

Observes a forty-five-year-old risk taker, "When people delay marriage, they get a chance to get to know themselves. You have to get to know yourself. When you finally realize who it is you are, you finally say, 'Hey, the lights went on. Somebody is home and this is who I am.' "

Just about anybody can get married. But a marriage has a better chance of success if you have already established your identity and priorities before you commit yourself to a relationship. Because as you develop, your needs in a partner are going to change. For instance, a woman who has started her own business has a different set of needs from a woman who is happily employed by a company. Says one such woman, "If I were with a man right now who understood employer/employee relationships and making the most of playing the corporate game, he would find me extremely frustrating." Instead of a corporate man, she has linked up with another entrepreneur. "We have so much in common," she notes. The man she would have selected five years ago when she was a happy employee might have been ill-equipped to deal with her in her new persona as an entrepreneur.

Marriages that occur prior to your finding your sense of direction undergo much more stress. The man you are married to may end up with a wife who is completely different from what he thought he was marrying. The easiest way to avoid a divorce—which is inconvenient and unpleasant—is to take your time getting married.

Moreover, after you have achieved success on your own, your reasons for marrying may be very different from what the previous generation's were. "The only reason I'd get married would be for love," says an entrepreneur. Indeed, as women have their own financial security, fewer and fewer marry for economic security. They marry for love, companionship, and the opportunity to share on an ongoing basis.

SCOLLARD'S LAW   You will be changed by your success. The person you become may want an entirely different husband from the one that appealed to you beforehand.

SCOLLARD'S LAW   Women's continuing growth frequently results in multiple marriages.

SCOLLARD'S LAW   Once you become successful, prenuptial agreements become even more important.

SUCCESS AND MARRIAGE

Success and marriage do not necessarily go hand in hand. Some husbands and lovers are jealous of success, preferring a woman who is insecure and less confident. It takes a special breed of man to accept a successful woman. The man must be secure within himself. It is easier usually if he's also successful himself.

Generally, successful risk takers are turned off by wimpy men. Since risk taking is a strong characteristic, wimpiness is eschewed. Probably you avoid any contact with weak, insecure men. Says one risk taker, "It's very difficult to work on a daily basis with indecisive men. They are wimps. I have no respect for them." She finally quit her job and started her own business so that she could deal with people she found more acceptable.

Some women have difficulty finding a strong man who can accept them for what they are. "Some men don't want the woman to be more successful than they are. They have problems with their own identity when a woman is highly successful," notes a top-ranked television producer. "I have trouble finding men that can keep my pace without feeling competitive," agrees advertising agency founder Rebecca Tilton.

Of course, women need to learn to be comfortable with their success themselves. One woman admits to "tremendous guilt" when her husband accompanied her to industry functions where she was highly recognized and no one even knew who he was.

But there are plenty of men who bask in their wives' success. One executive who is the only woman in senior management at a large corporation is routinely accompanied by her husband to corporate meetings where spouses are included. He spends the days with the wives. He's delightful, and they look forward to his company at the fashion shows and tours typically designed for wives. He serves as a goodwill ambassador for his wife, since she is beautiful and were it not for her charming husband, the wives might be inclined to be threatened by and suspicious of her.

As a successful risk taker you simply have to search for men who like successful women. This is easier if you look and act like the success that you are. If men can immediately discern that you are successful, you won't have to waste your time with those who can't handle a successful woman. If they can tell it from the first, they will avoid you and you'll only be approached by the ones who enjoy what you have become.

SCOLLARD'S LAW Being successful and being feminine are not mutually exclusive.

SCOLLARD'S LAW Just because you give orders all day at the office doesn't mean you have to give orders in bed.

9

What to Do if
You Fail

THE PRESSURE when you take a risk is for the risk to produce a favorable outcome. You try not to fall short or be disappointed. You strive to achieve your goals.

To consider failure, we must understand its antithesis: Success. Exactly what is success? Is it money? Family? Personal happiness? Is it all of these three? Can you fail in one area and still be a success? Says Susan Kudla Finn, Executive Director of American Women in Radio and Television and a partner at Smith Bucklin in Washington, D.C., "Failure means not living up to your potential. It doesn't mean making mistakes. Failure is not learning from them."

Continues Finn, "Society views failure as a matter of money earned or money lost. If you're a business failure, you declare bankruptcy. I see failure in terms of personal bankruptcy, of selling out to gain power and prestige and using yourself, your family, and your friends as collateral. That's the worst kind of bankruptcy." She cites a woman whom she considers to be in moral bankruptcy: She sacrificed friendships for her career. And propositioned a friend's husband because she thought he had the power to help her with her career.

Certainly Finn is right. Without your personal integrity intact, *success* or *failure* are meaningless terms. The most important thing is to preserve yourself and achieve certain goals at the same time.

Says Tina Potter, an entrepreneur based in Houston, "Success is being who I am and being able to achieve something. The financial rewards validate the fact that I have a creative mind that also functions on the bottom line in a financial way. Being creative is exciting, but it has to make money." She agrees that integrity is essential to success. "I would rather not have money and be honest than have money and be dishonest."

But since we control our lives, we can choose to maintain our integrity and achieve financial goals, too.

If you have a job, success means moving up the corporate ladder, getting more responsibility—and a bigger paycheck. "Failure means not making it, not getting promotions," says Merry Clark, who works for Hearst Corporation. "Women don't behave professionally enough. They don't talk or act executive. You have to act and think like a man. You fail when you get pegged, doing something like crying. Certain behavior mistakes make it easy for men to peg you. Sleeping around—men can do it, but women can't. Getting emotional—you have to fight back on their level. You have to play the game to succeed in a corporation."

SCOLLARD'S LAW Financial gain and integrity are not mutually exclusive.

BUSINESS FAILURE

Business failures are quite permissible. Our society has legitimized it and provided a structure for failure. We have chapter 2 and chapter 7 in case worse comes to worse. The saga of much-failed business people who finally succeed constitutes the lore of our business mythology. We love stories like that of R. H. Macy, who failed seven times before he finally launched the successful New York store.

The bigger the failure, the smaller the stigma. If you build a large business and it fails, there is virtually no personal loss of face. Whereas if you have a fledgling business that goes under, your personal credibility is damaged. If you fail big, as did the Hunt brothers when they tried to corner the entire world silver market, you lose no face and gain substantial notoriety.

SCOLLARD'S LAW   The bigger the failure, the better.

SPORTS ANALOGY

America worships at the shrine of sports competitions—in which someone must always lose. There is no stigma in losing—unless you lose all the time. "It's not whether you win or lose, but how you play the game" is a much-mouthed cliché.

Indeed, there is little stigma in losing if you win sometimes. And winning is not everything—although we adore our heroes who manage to win a great deal.

Sports competition is interesting because it is a reflection of training and effort. You give your best, and if you lose, it is not that you didn't try hard enough, it's that your competition was capable of doing better than you.

The biggest competition in sports is with yourself. You push your limits and your endurance and you can measure how well you do. Do you run seven-minute miles or three-minute ones? You can see physical indicators of improvement, of your slack or effort. Whether your golf handicap is 3 or 21, it is a reflection not only of your natural ability but of how much effort you expend on the game.

Thus, if you do your best and you still lose in a sport, you nevertheless have the feeling that you did the best you could do. If someone runs five-minute miles and your best speed is seven minutes, you know in advance that you are unlikely to win.

You might think that sports would provide a model for winning and losing in other parts of our culture. Since we win and lose in sports, you might say, why shouldn't we view other risk taking in the same light?

The sports analogy does not hold up for two reasons. In other aspects of life (a) the risk is not as well defined nor the rehearsal as direct; and (b) the measurement of your best effort is not possible.

When you prepare for a sports competition, your goals are clearly defined: to beat the tennis pro in straight sets or to outpace your aerobics instructor. You can measure your risks. And you can prepare for them by performing certain tasks repeatedly. So that when the day of the actual competition arrives, you have prepared yourself.

The preparation for the risks you take in the rest of your life are in no way as tidy. How do you prepare for marriage? How do you prepare to start a business in a market that has been previously untapped?

You do the best you can. To prepare for marriage, for instance, first of all by dating a lot of different people and spending as much time as possible with your prospective groom. But nothing can precisely prepare you for your marriage—which is why marriages fail. With a new business, you may work for someone else for years and research and prepare for a new venture to the best of your ability, but nothing can prepare you for the vagaries of the marketplace.

But the key element that separates the other risks in life from the risks you take in sports has to do with your ability to measure your best effort. In sports, you can time yourself to prove that you ran faster than you ever ran before—even if you lost the marathon. You can measure your golf game, your tennis game. This way you can be satisfied with your performance in sports even if you lose the competition.

This is not the case with your personal and business lives. You cannot measure whether you gave it your best. Moreover, you may not have made the right moves to salvage the situation. You can tell when your backhand is weak in tennis, but it's hard to gauge your management strengths on the day you get fired. There are no videotapes to help you study your faulty game.

In short, you can fail in sports and your self-esteem will still be intact. If you fail in business or your personal life, it can be shattering. It is not that society punishes us for failing—we punish ourselves. We doubt ourselves. We are embarrassed by our performance, by our inability to achieve what we aimed to achieve.

Much of the rigidity by which we judge ourselves can be attributed to Calvinism. When things go wrong, it is as though God has given up on us. Or worse, that it was God's Will that we failed. We take it personally. It is as though we are being banished from the Garden of Eden.

Interestingly, the more blessed you are, the greater the shame of your failure. If you have everything, go to the best schools, have the best job opportunities, and are set off on the fast track, society is much more interested in your failure. It is as though you have no permission to fail. You had everything going for you, so how could you not succeed? On the other hand, if you had to struggle against the odds, if you are a blue-collar worker and are not "one of God's Chosen" and you fail, it's okay. The feeling is that you were not destined for success in the first place.

SCOLLARD'S LAW   We need to give ourselves permission to fail.

WOMEN AND FAILURE

When women fail, it is viewed differently from when men fail. First of all, the signals are different. We fall into that group that is not "God's Chosen People." When we fail, society is more likely to say, "Of course she failed. No woman could do that." Since society expects less from us—especially in business—there was far less confidence in our ability to succeed in the first place. So our failure comes as no surprise.

Our society expects more of men—particularly in business.

In our personal lives the opposite is often true. If our marriages fail, the stigma is worse for the woman. If a man is "no fun to live with," he's regarded as a benign challenge for his wife. If she's hard to live with, she's a bitch and he was right to leave her.

With our children, the men are credited with their successes and we usually get the blame for their mistakes. We take Johnny to Little League three times a week for ten years, and when he makes the team, he's a "chip off the old man's block." If he gets arrested, suddenly it's not just Tom's kid; it's Tom and Judy's kid. And Judy probably spent too much time playing tennis and not enough attention to the kids.

The good news is that we women are less devastated by failure than men. "Men give themselves a hard time for failing to meet unrealistically maintained standards," observes psychiatrist Ralph Hirschowitz. "They don't give themselves much permission. Women are easier on themselves when they fail."

Women tend to judge what is possible more accurately. Moreover, since self-esteem problems are a major weakness of our sex in this society, we may well have not set very high expectations for ourselves in the first place. This is one of the reasons why women's businesses tend to be small. Very often women don't dare to be big. They're thrilled with small success. Since we take smaller risks, we usually have smaller failures.

When I interviewed some of the most successful women in our culture, they told me, "I never expected to be so successful." On the other hand, I've never had a successful businessman say that to me.

In summary, when we fail, society is likely to be snide in its assessment of our capabilities. But we are far less likely to punish ourselves as severely as our male counterparts.

SCOLLARD'S LAW   Expect great success.

MISTAKES

Mistakes are much less serious than failures. A mistake can be rectified. A failure is definite. The damage is greater. The recovery time is longer.

A mistake is an error of judgment. A failure is an all-out effort that did not succeed.

A mistake can be based on carelessness or ignorance. A failure is the result of planning and strategy that did not succeed, that did not produce the desired result.

A mistake can be put to rights with a note or a phone call; face may not even be lost. A failure requires rebuilding; even your credibility has been damaged.

SCOLLARD'S LAW   Be sensitive to your mistakes and you can avert failure.

FAILURE:
Mistakes and Creativity

Some of the greatest people in Western civilization have been considered failures by most of their peers. Particularly the creative members of our society. The artist Vincent van Gogh, for instance, was widely regarded as a failure. The poet Ezra Pound. Jesus was regarded as a failure, crucified between two thieves. Some of our creative geniuses have only been vindicated by history.

Consider the role of failure and mistakes in the creative process. Whenever anyone is attempting to create something new, fresh, or different, she risks failure. Or, at the very least, she risks making a mistake. If creative people did not give themselves permission to fail, they would never take the leap of faith necessary whenever new and different things are tried.

The point here is the necessity of believing in yourself. Sometimes you can be right and the rest of your generation wrong. Your peers may say you failed, but time will vindicate you.

SCOLLARD'S LAW   You must have strong self-esteem to be successfully creative.

PERSISTENCE

Our society is very interesting. It may demonstrate the same morbid curiosity in failure as the general public does in a gory automobile accident. But it loves a comeback. Our real heroes are the ones we have watched crash and return as phoenixes from their own ashes.

What is unacceptable in our society are the failures that quit. The bums on Skid Row. People who fail and have no desire to come back.

What we love to see are persistent, determined people who fail, admit their failure, and try again. Persistence is the American ideal.

We love the tales. Richard Nixon, who was defeated in so many elections before he won the presidency, who was downed in Watergate and came back to be one of our elder statesmen. We vote for people who fail. We admire their tenacity. We don't hold failure against them. It works for them.

We love people who try and try again and finally win. For instance, Kaye Lani Rae Rafko, Miss America in 1988, did not coast into her position without some real setbacks. She was in beauty competitions for several years prior to winning. Initially she did well. Then she had two years where she won nothing. "People would say, 'Why doesn't she just give up? She doesn't have what it takes. She's over the hill.' There were times when I didn't even make the top five out of nine contestants," recalls the beauty queen. At one point she was booed when she was onstage. "I really had an attitude that I'm proud of myself and who I've come to be and I'm not going to let anyone stand in my way. My motto is: Hard work and perseverance pay off."

When we see people who've failed and come back, we see part of ourselves. Because we all make mistakes. Most of us experience at least one failure in our lives. And it keeps us running scared. "The pressure of not succeeding is always there," says an entrepreneur.

A male entrepreneur says he views failure positively: "Failure is the energy upon which everything is built."

SCOLLARD'S LAW Failure is what you make of it. Why not make it the cornerstone of your next success?

HOW TO STAGE YOUR COMEBACK

There is an unspoken etiquette of failure. First of all, you should admit that you've failed. This contrition is taken as being humbled by the experience, "of having learned a good lesson." To admit that you have failed is beside the point, because the tom-toms of the business community have telegraphed your setbacks to your competitors before you have had time even to call your husband to give him the bad news. Bad news travels fast.

Next, you should itemize the mistakes that you've made. Ideally these admissions should be made to all the people who were giving you advice that turned out to be correct, which unfortunately you did not heed. Be prepared to hear, "I told you so." These public acts of humility begin the forgiveness process of your peers. Humility is the beginning of rebuilding your credibility. Your eating humble pie is initially a source of glee to your detractors, but after a while the thrill is gone, and public opinion turns in your favor.

Smile. Under no circumstances let anyone see you cry. Do not avoid people. Face the world and as quickly as possible put your failure behind you.

After you've said your mea culpas, act as though it never occurred. Begin the rebuilding process as quickly as possible. But keep a low profile. This is not a time for bragging or bravado. You should be unassuming and don your sackcloth and ashes until you have something substantial to show.

Then never mention your failure again until you achieve new success. At that time remind the newspaper reporters. They will love your story of hard times. And finally, you will be a real heroine.

SCOLLARD'S LAW Comebacks are admired more than those who make success look very easy.

REASONS FOR FAILURE

Failure can often be avoided. The reasons are quite simple. One good thing to note is that you can learn from other people's failures. You don't have to make all of the mistakes yourself.

Some of the reasons why you fail in business have to do with your attitude. Some of the reasons are fundamental business errors due to poor judgment, oversight, and carelessness. Big Picture problems, such as a sudden reversal in the economy or pestilence and plague, are usually not the cause for career setbacks. The reasons for most failures in risk taking are avoidable, controllable reasons.

Arrogance. Overestimating your own capabilities is a serious error. Some of the more spectacular failures come from people who started out well. "Success can be more dangerous than adversity," notes New York executive Judith Moncrieff. Some people's careers start out extremely well. They are promoted and rewarded. But they come to a point where they start believing their own press: They think they can do no wrong. They start throwing their weight around, being a little careless. They may speak out of turn to someone superior. They make one too many enemies. And one day they are fired. Or one day the competition moves in.

It is important to keep both feet on the ground. If everyone you know tells you how marvelous you are all the time, you're surrounding yourself with the wrong people. You need some friends in your life who will speak their minds to you instead of simply praising you when things are going great.

Part of arrogance is inflating your view of yourself and underestimating the capabilities of your competition. There are a lot of smart people, and one of them might open a competing shop across the street. Pay attention. Take other people seriously. It's not just the smartest but the most effective who succeed.

Worry. If you have self-esteem problems and seriously doubt yourself, you may be your own worst enemy. You need to develop a sense of reality so that you can tell what to worry about and what things will be okay. If you cannot gain perspective, you may be paralyzed into inaction.

At the most extreme, one executive relates that a man in her office who worried about everything, took everything personally, and was paranoid, ultimately committed suicide.

Worry is a way of creating stress for yourself. Study chapter 6 about dealing with stress to help put your worry under control.

Self-knowledge. You have to know what you want before you can have it. If you do not have an understanding of your priorities and the things that make you happy, you are likely to be miserable.

Most things do not just come to you. You have to bring them into your life. Be honest with yourself about what makes you happy. If you are not, and are doing things you do not enjoy, you are less likely to succeed. Indeed, you might welcome failure because it frees you from a situation that makes you very unhappy.

Knowing the Rules. The only way to succeed in corporate life is to play the game the way the men wrote it. Says executive Merry Clark, "Women's lack of knowledge of corporate life is the toughest hurdle they face. They don't know the rules of the game. Women have to learn." Clark suggests women find a mentor—male or female—who will coach them through the political minefields of corporate life.

Being excellent is not enough in itself to guarantee success in traditional male-dominated corporate America. Gamesmanship is essential.

Delegating. "Innovative people don't like to manage and often won't hire anyone who can," observes stockmarket guru Steve Leuthold, who spends much of his life observing management. The lack of management has caused some spectacular disasters.

Recognize that unless your firm is very small and you are exceptionally talented, you cannot do everything yourself. Hire people with complementary strengths.

Unrealistic Expectations. One woman who considered herself a failure in one of her jobs later recognized that the job had been undoable. Neither she nor her employer had created a realistic set of objectives.

Often people punish themselves as though they had failed when their mistake was the same: They had set out to do the undoable. This can be extraordinarily frustrating for overachieving can-do people. One woman told me she had practically self-destructed trying to accomplish an impossible assignment.

Keep an open mind when you approach new projects. Leave open the possibility that the job may not be a viable alternative. Leave yourself flexible to walk away before you exhaust yourself attempting to do the impossible.

Also, make sure that you have a realistic time frame in which to complete projects. One woman sewed for twenty-four hours to cover a couch and make fifteen pillows for a showroom. She was sick for three days afterward. Instead of agreeing to meet that deadline, she should have either negotiated with the showroom for more time or hired someone to help her.

Business Divorces. Many businesses fail because they are partnerships and the partnerships don't work out. There is no more bitter acrimony and ill feeling in the aftermath of a business divorce than you'll see at the dissolution of many marriages.

Be slow to enter into a partnership. Most partnerships fail. Don't assume yours will be the exception to the rule. If you're starting a company, it can only have one boss: you. People usually enter partnerships for advice or moral support, but the partnership is usually a lousy solution. If you need moral support, get it from your friends on the side or join business associations. If you need advice, pay an adviser. If you need someone to make your decisions for you, you have no business being self-employed.

If you are determined to have a partnership, negotiate the contract at the very beginning, before you structure any kind of a deal. Negotiate it as you would a prenuptial agreement, when the bloom is on the rose and you're still speaking to each other. Cover yourself in case you disagree or one of you gets sick or dies. Carefully structure your partnership agreement. Chances are you will be using it.

Overspending. Sometimes people get successful and get carried away with spending. Success is fickle, it's important to continue to budget when times are good. "I see people spend, spend, spend," notes an Ohio-based entrepreneur. "People think you can relax when you start making money, but you can't. If you don't control your inventory and your spending, you are risking failure."

Borrowing too much money is a way of overspending. People say you are better off using somebody else's money to finance your growth. But it's important to remember you have to pay it back someday. Even if the banks want to loan you money—and they usually don't unless you don't need it—be cautious about dipping into the till. You have to repay not only the loan but the interest too.

Overexpansion. Once you have a business going, it's tempting to either duplicate it or expand. But it's important to recognize two things: First, not all businesses do as well large as they do small. Sometimes being small is an important part of their cachet. One woman says she found that thirty-two was the perfect number of employees for her design firm. Once she had thirty-eight she started losing the personal touch that her clients valued. She cut back to thirty-two. Many businesses have a magic size past which they should not grow. Be sensitive to this possibility.

Second, do not underestimate the amount of work entailed in expansion. Rosemary Garbett, who has ten restaurants and some related food businesses in Houston, advises, "If you expand, you've got to be a working owner. You can't let somebody run it for you. Nobody cares about your money like you do."

Details. The secret of success in smaller businesses is the attention to detail. It's important to know where you are making a sizable profit and where you are losing money. One woman who runs a sizable bakery discovered only by accident, when she brought in an accountant for another purpose, that her biggest-selling pie was costing her money. It was not profitable. She raised the price and is even considering discontinuing the product.

You must understand every financial aspect of your business to ensure its survival. Says restaurateur Garbett, "I sign every check, I sign every invoice. I am here a lot."

REASONS FOR FAILURES

1. *Arrogance*—When you are riding high, you may be riding for a fall.
2. *Worry*—Only worry about what you can control. Otherwise you can paralyze yourself.
3. *Self-knowledge*—No one is going to tell you what makes you happy. But if your work does not, you are less likely to succeed.
4. *Knowing the rules*—Women will never make it to the top in corporate America unless they learn the rules of the corporate game—and play them as well as men.
5. *Unrealistic expectations*—Trying to do the impossible is enormously frustrating. The hard part is deciding what is possible and what is not.
6. *Business divorces*—Most partnerships fail. Avoid them.
7. *Overspending*—Even when things look rosy, save money for a rainy day.
8. *Overexpansion*—Is bigger better? And can you manage it?
9. *Details*—The nitty-gritty of a business is often the secret of its success.

LESSONS FROM FAILURES

When you fail, you must analyze the reasons for it. This is where self-honesty is important. You must be absolutely candid in your analysis of the failure. Where did you make your first mistake? What could you have done to correct it? Where did you make your second mistake? Where was your judgment wrong? What could you have done to avert it?

Failure can be turned into a positive experience. Entrepreneur Sam Metters has a very positive attitude about it. "It is because you fail that you keep going. If I had never failed, I would never have examined who I am, where I want to go, and how I plan to get there. If I were to succeed, I'd never have to examine my weakness and my strength. And therefore I'd never really know myself and my potential. Failure is a necessary milestone in the evolution of growth."

It is important to turn failure into something positive, notes a woman who has experienced a series of misfortunes. "It is negative unless you make good out of it. Then it becomes a sacrament. You can change it from a sacrifice into a sacrament," she says.

The most important thing you learn is never to make that specific mistake again. "You have to resolve that you will learn from your mistakes," notes executive Merry Clark. "You have to turn a failure into your next success. Once you make a mistake in a corporation, you are doomed unless you can turn it around," she advises. "If you can't, leave."

All mistakes are not fatal. But some people never learn. Some people fail because of a personal shortcoming. They may change the product and restructure the company or get a totally different job, depending on their circumstances. But if the fault is a character deficiency, unless they come to grips with their problem, they will make the same mistake again and again.

Caution. Failure almost always makes you more cautious. So often, having done your homework more thoroughly could have averted a major setback. "You learn to try a different type of risk taking," suggests entrepreneur Pam Fletcher-Hafemann. "You learn not to rush into things."

Usually there is no reason to rush into things. You should give yourself a year to find a new job or a year to investigate a new company idea. Impatience is a major reason for failure. And failure is a great teacher of caution.

SCOLLARD'S LAW   Act in haste. Repent at leisure.

Humility. Mistakes keep you humble. And humility is an important aspect of keeping perspective. A clear perspective is one of the most important assets you can have.

You can't be too humble. It is attractive and it is useful.

SCOLLARD'S LAW We must have been meant to be humble, or life wouldn't give us so many opportunities to humble ourselves.

Compassion. One of the things you learn from making big mistakes is an understanding of what other people suffer. A major failure opens your eyes to humankind. You suddenly understand why some people never recover from failure. How easy it would be just to quit and be defeated by life.

You appreciate the obstacles people overcome to be successful. It broadens your humanness and kindness—and makes you a better boss and competitor.

After all, one of the objectives of taking risks is to improve the quality of your life. And the quality of your life would be very poor if you did not have great respect for other people.

SCOLLARD'S LAW Compassion is the gentlest of passions.

Communication. Lack of communication is a major reason for failure. Even those who consider themselves masters at interaction make the most fundamental communication mistakes. When in doubt, clarify. Follow up spoken agreements with a letter. Make every effort to keep the lines of communication open. Business is a quintessentially social act.

Don't assume that something is understood. Be specific. Be accessible so that people feel free to tell you bad news, to keep you informed.

SCOLLARD'S LAW You cannot be successful in isolation.

LEARN FROM FAILURE

With a positive attitude, the most dismal failure can be turned around into an important learning experience and a new beginning. You learn things you might not learn otherwise. You have an excellent opportunity to evaluate your friendships. You find out who your true friends are—the others are nowhere in sight.

Your good-time buddies don't return your phone calls and won't meet you for lunch. Only your real friends support you through your bleakest hours. One of the advantages of failure is learning what friendship can be all about.

You can learn things about yourself you might not ever be forced to accept otherwise. You learn the importance of rapid recuperation and private tears. You learn how to reach down into yourself and pull out ribbons of inner strength you never imagined you had. And those ribbons turn into steel.

You learn that all the fears of failure you had when you were taking risks were exaggerated. You can survive anything.

SCOLLARD'S LAW   Just because you make a mistake doesn't mean you *are* one.

ADVANTAGES OF FAILURE

1. You find out who your friends are.
2. You discover the extent of your resilience.
3. You are forced to accept your limitations.
4. You can relax. You don't have to keep up with the Joneses, because you can't.
5. You no longer have to butter up your boss.
6. You have increased freedom.
7. You can redefine yourself. You can reconsider your options.
8. Anywhere is UP.
9. Reality is clearer. Your perspective changes. Your success may have distorted your view.
10. You can start from the beginning again.

Index